BASICS

DESIGN

01

Format

Gavin Ambrose
Paul Harris

2nd edition

WITHDRAWN

Ethical: aware
ness/
reflect
ion/
debate

D1145787

a
va
academia

An AVA Book
Published by AVA Publishing SA
Rue des Fontenailles 16
Case Postale
1000 Lausanne 6
Switzerland
Tel: +41 786 005 109
Email: enquiries@avabooks.com

Distributed by Thames & Hudson (ex-North America)
181a High Holborn
London WC1V 7QX
United Kingdom
Tel: +44 20 7845 5000
Fax: +44 20 7845 5055
Email: sales@thameshudson.co.uk
www.thamesandhudson.com

Distributed in the USA & Canada by:
Ingram Publisher Services Inc.
1 Ingram Blvd.
La Vergne TN 37086
USA
Tel: +1 866 400 5351
Fax: +1 800 838 1149
Email: customer.service@ingrampublisherservices.com

English Language Support Office
AVA Publishing (UK) Ltd.
Tel: +44 1903 204 455
Email: enquiries@avabooks.com

Second edition © AVA Publishing SA 2012
First published in 2004

All rights reserved. No part of this publication may be reproduced,
stored in a retrieval system or transmitted in any form or by any means,
electronic, mechanical, photocopying, recording or otherwise, without
permission of the copyright holder.

ISBN 978-2-940411-79-5

Library of Congress Cataloging-in-Publication Data
Ambrose, Gavin; Harris, Paul, 1971-.
Basics Design 01: Format. / Gavin Ambrose; Paul Harris. p. cm.
Includes bibliographical references and index.
ISBN: 9782940411795 (pbk. :alk. paper)
eISBN: 9782940447329
1. Books -- Format. 2. Graphic design (Typography).
Z246 .A53 2012

10 9 8 7 6 5 4 3 2 1

Design and text by Gavin Ambrose and Paul Harris
Original photography by Xavier Young

Production by AVA Book Production Pte. Ltd., Singapore
Tel: +65 6334 8173
Fax: +65 6259 9830
Email: production@avabooks.com.sg

R. Newbold

Designed by Aboud Creative, this brochure for a clothing range by R. Newbold comprises a 42-page section printed in four special colours – black, silver, blue and yellow – rather than the normal process colours. All the images appear as duotones of silver and black. Bound into a hard cover, a die-cut large square creates a uniquely shaped publication.

Client: R. Newbold
Design: Aboud Creative
Process: 42-page section, four special colours litho, bound into a hard cover and die cut

Contents

Contents

Introduction

Modern designers have a multitude of tools at their disposal with which to create printed matter that communicates effectively. Layout, typography, colour and images are all critical in differentiating one design from another and relaying information, but an often underrated and underused tool is that of format itself, the physical presence of the piece.

We are all familiar with a wide range of formats, mainly for ergonomic reasons: a poster needs to be large enough to be read from a distance; a stamp needs to be small enough to fit on an envelope; a book needs to be big enough for text to print at a readable size, but small enough to be held comfortably in the hand. Because of its almost exclusively utilitarian nature, and due to the use of many generic formats, format can therefore sometimes be overlooked by designers.

Yet, the format of a piece of design provides a physical point of contact with the user that crucially affects how users receive the printed or online communication. In this fully revised and updated second edition, featuring a broad range of exemplary design work, interviews and design activities, we explore how you can play with format to maximum effect in your own projects. Even though printed matter is often predisposed to be of a certain size, shape, extent and weight, we will look at how you can use format to vary these elements and so vitally add an extra dimension to your own design work.

Purpose and narrative
A range of formats serve different purposes depending on the content of something. A narrative serves to entertain or inform readers by telling them a story.

Printed media
A whole myriad of different printed and on-screen formats exists. From traditional posters to emerging technologies and media, format offers a range of choices that affect the final outcome.

Construction
A range of print-finishing techniques enable a humble piece of paper to be folded, cut, glued and formed to create magnificent printed outcomes.

Identity and branding
The way in which we use format can create a sense of branding and identity in printed materials. Be it through stock choices, print finishing or colour, a sense of identity can be instilled and developed.

Shape and form
In many instances, the shape and form of a printed piece extends into the realm of art – and so allows us to appreciate it more as an object than as a mere instrument of communication.

New media
On-screen formats do not need to be restricted by screen dimensions. A variety of techniques can be employed to use space creatively, such as pop-up boxes, animations and innovative navigation.

Client: Canal Building

Design: Cartlidge Levene

Process: Self-containing two-
section brochure, printed on
silk stock and uncoated stock

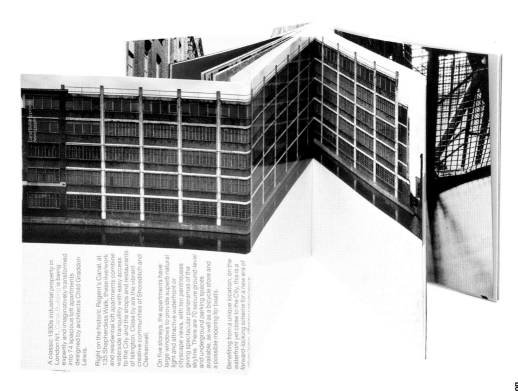

A classic 1930s industrial property in London N1, Canal Building is being expertly and imaginatively transformed into 74 spacious loft apartments designed by architects Child Graddon Lewis.

Right on the historic Regent's Canal, at 135 Shepherdess Walk, these live/work and residential loft apartments combine waterside tranquility with easy access to the City and the shops and restaurants of Islington. Close by are the vibrant creative communities of Shoreditch and Clerkenwell.

On five storeys, the apartments have large windows to provide superb natural light and attractive waterfront or cityscape views, with ten penthouses giving spectacular panoramas of the skyline. There are 70 secure ground-level and underground parking spaces available, as well as a bicycle store and a possible mooring for boats.

Benefiting from a unique location, on the waterfront yet close to the City, this is a forward-looking scheme for a new era of

Introduction

Canal Building

Created by Cartlidge Levene for the Canal Building in Shepherdess Walk, London, this brochure was designed to promote the loft-style development of a formerly derelict building. Made from two sections, one comprises 84 pages printed on a silk stock with commissioned imagery of the surrounding area; the other section is printed on an uncoated stock and contains building plans and other details. The last page of the first section wraps around to form a cover for the whole publication. This piece acts both as a means of communication, utilizing the innovative format to divide information, and also as a symbol of the design values of the development.

Client: Melt London
Design: Agitprop
Process: Six-panel concertina
fold, die cut and supported
by two hardback boards
sealed by a rubber band

Chapter 1
Purpose and narrative

When selecting an appropriate format for a design, there are two distinct parts of the design that need to be considered. Firstly, there is its 'purpose'. What is it for? Secondly, there is its meaning or 'narrative'.

All designs need to address these two distinct facets with equal vigour. As a designer, you need to consider the purpose that your design will serve, and any special considerations this will entail. Does the design need to protect something fragile? Are there restrictions placed on production costs? Are there specific reasons why certain substrates and materials may not be appropriate? But design is also about telling a story. It is about conveying information or values about a product or service. Choice of format can have an impact on this, affecting how we perceive a brand or design.

'Design is a plan for arranging elements in such a way as best to accomplish a particular purpose.'

Charles Eames

Melt London

Agitprop based this mailer for fashion label Melt London on a six-panel concertina fold. To convert it into a mailer, two semicircles were die cut on the vertical sides of the piece to allow boards to be held in place, front and back, by a rubber band. The binding device is pragmatic – it is designed to contain a set of images. But it also conveys a story or narrative and a picture of a modern, clean brand with a sense of fun. Internally, the folds of the concertina feature images that convey a sequential narrative; altering the pace, pattern and colour of these helps to pace the story.

Client: Iceland
Design: Iris Associates
Process: Polystyrene-formed
package for mailing book
and product

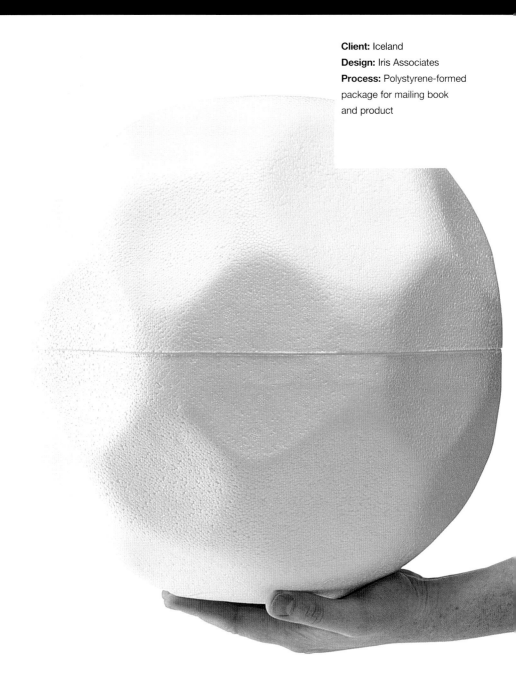

Containment and protection

A major element of design is to contain and protect the object or function for which it was created. This can be in the form of a simple book, where the pages are bound (contained) into an outer cover (protection). We will now look at some of the many creative ways this can be achieved.

Iceland

Iris Associates created something extraordinary for UK food retailer Iceland's mailer to journalists. Not happy to merely produce a brochure and showcase CD to advertise their Christmas food range, the studio packaged the contents of the mailer in a snowball that received extensive coverage in both consumer and design media.

Containment and protection

Client: Making
Space Publishers
Design: SAS
Process: 21 A2 posters
contained in polypropylene
silk-screened bag

Making Space Publishers

Designed by SAS for an exhibition entitled 'Inside Cover', this catalogue challenges the traditional brochure format. Rather than bind the pages into a coherent whole, they are instead collated into a bag that closes with press studs. The titles of the posters are printed on the outside fold edge so that they can be easily identified when stacked. Each poster features an exhibit of a participating designer or artist.

In Feburary 1979 The Clash set off on their first American tour.

Caroline: Part of the punk ethic was to refuse to be in any way gracious to anyone from the record company who came backstage. My charm helped a bit, especially when we ran out of money halfway through the tour, and I had to go on my knees to the record company and ask for more cash to finish the tour. But they did it because The Clash were playing fantastic gigs that were absolute sell-outs.

You have to understand that The Clash never ever did a gig that wasn't rampacked. From the first gig they ever did in London. Because of the build-up, with everyone knowing there was something happening. Unlike the Pistols who for the first few gigs were building the punk audience. By the time The Clash came along there was already quite a big scene, so they never ever had to do a gig where they had to win over the audience. The audience was so ready and up for it. I don't think there's been any band in the history of rock'n'roll that has had that experience. Even the Beatles, the Rolling Stones had to build an audience. But the audience was there for The Clash, ready for it.

Bob: The Clash liked America in general. Coming from England, the whole country seems like Disneyland. That's what America does well: we are big and bright and candy-coloured and pink and yellow and "red, white and blue". You come to America and it's fast food and fast girls and fast cars and big, wide-open streets. In America anyone says anything to anybody - pretty loudly. The band really liked that swaggering American attitude and the big cars.

Client: Vision On Publishing
Design: Form®
Process: Four-colour edition-bound book in slipcase

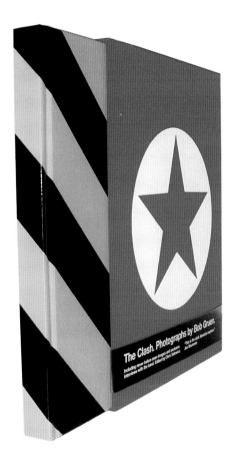

The Clash. Photographs by Bob Gruen.

Including never before seen images and exclusive interviews with the band. Edited by Chris Salewicz.

"This is the stuff. Absolutely magical." Joe Strummer

Vision On Publishing

For this book, featuring photographs by Bob Gruen of seminal punk band The Clash, the cover is decorated with industrial warning chevrons in keeping with the direct nature of the music The Clash produced. Inside the book, the chevrons provide a strong visual frame for the images contained within it. Form gave the product extra durability by including a slipcase to store and protect it.

Slipcases

A slipcase is generally a box structure made from a hard and durable substrate to contain and protect a book, or to group several books together in one package. A slipcase also adds another element to the presentation of the product. It is open at one end so that the book's spine is visible and will naturally have slightly bigger dimensions than the items it is to contain, which are designed to fit snugly inside.

Woven

Woven is a trend-forecast book for the fashion and textile industry. This edition is a loose-leaf binder contained in a cloth-covered box, which is printed inside with the face of the cover model throughout the pages of the book. This allows the files to be contained, but also allows for them to be altered, changed or added to in the future.

Client: *Woven*
Design: MadeThought
Process: Four colour
and spot varnish, in box with
printed inners with block
colour and spot varnish overlay

Containment and protection | Storytelling

Storytelling

Many formats offer a fixed narrative. Books, for instance, have a start, middle and an end, which are usually fixed in order by binding. Designers can use this intrinsic order and pace to convey stories and narratives – arguably the key to graphic design.

'To design is to communicate clearly by whatever means you can control or master.'

Milton Glaser

MoDo Papers

Designers use a wide range of substrates in brochure design to harness the diverse textures and tactile qualities available, or to benefit from the superior printability of some paper grades, as this brochure called 'London: cloudy' by SEA Design for the paper manufacturer MoDo illustrates. The designers were ultimately trying to engage with print buyers so needed to create something intriguing. The dramatic photography of Richard Green fulfils this narrative role and creates a point of interest to engage with the viewer, while also reflecting the qualities of the textured stocks.

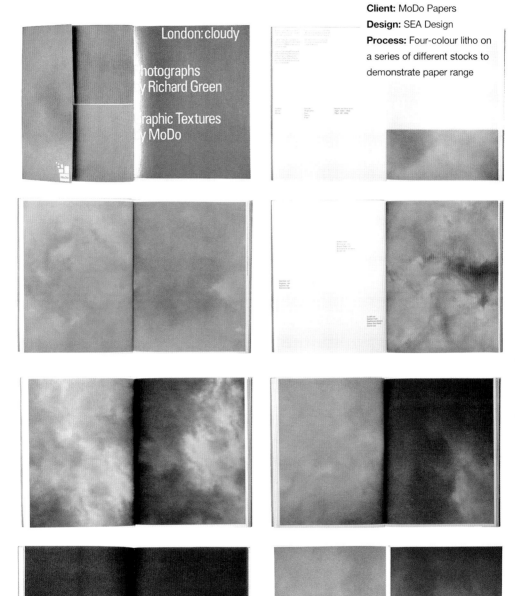

Client: MoDo Papers
Design: SEA Design
Process: Four-colour litho on a series of different stocks to demonstrate paper range

Containment and protection | **Storytelling** | Form follows function

Kick *ass*

In 1994, Chloë Sevigny was hailed 'the coolest girl in the world' by author Jay McInerney. Now, between her long-running role in Big Love and cult clothing line for Opening Ceremony, the 36 year-old proves she's still an avatar of East Coast cool. Here, the indie star reflects on the meaning of rebellion – now and then.

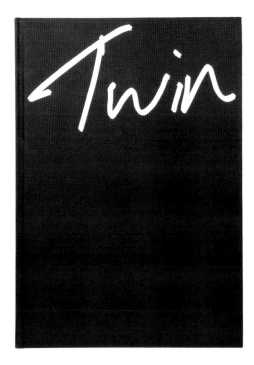

Twin Magazine

Twin Magazine is a cloth-bound, hard-backed biannual that showcases art, culture and feminist features alongside commissioned fashion photography. Each page tells a story by using contrasting poster typefaces, a consistency of style-centred text and bold fashion photography.

Twin Magazine uses an amalgamation of different formats to present its photographs, giving the magazine pace. Passepartouts and full-bleed images are used throughout, encouraging readers to focus on each page before continuing onwards with the story.

Client: *Twin Magazine*
Design: Planning Unit
Process: Magazine using a
series of design elements to
create a narrative

Rebel
girls

*Amidst sweeping political change in the
Middle East, Britain's youth have been
valiantly fighting their own political
corner in a no less important plight.
Protest and activism have become the
watchwords of a generation previously
branded apolitical. From this year
of discontent has emerged one of the
most politically charged sets of citizens
since the Sixties. Only this time around
revolution has a distinctly female face.
Twin meets the teenage footsoldiers who
are fighting for their rights.*

jennifer

17 years old, Cambridge

Form follows function

It is commonly held that design has two discrete functions – its form and its function. A design's form is the physical manifestion, while its function is what it is trying to communicate. Ultimately, some of the best designs occur when form and function merge seamlessly together, creating a solution that is greater than the sum of its parts.

'Form follows function – that has been misunderstood. Form and function should be one, joined in a spiritual union.'
Frank Lloyd Wright

McNaughton Paper

To demonstrate the ability to print on a new, high-quality transparent paper, Roundel created this brochure for the paper company McNaughton. The humorous design uses the transparency of the stock to juxtapose an image printed in orange onto photographs by John Edwards that appear on facing pages: by turning the trace-link page, a jelly mould becomes a swimmer's hat (top), a tightrope becomes a washing line (middle) and a candle flame becomes a water droplet (bottom).

Client: McNaughton Paper
Design: Roundel
Process: 17-page loose-leaf
sheet brochure with tracing
paper dust jacket

 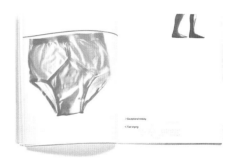

Client: UBS Investment Bank
Design: Radley Yeldar
Process: Die-cut invitation

Private \

UBS Investment Bank

Die cuts are a simple yet highly effective mechanism for creating a dramatic and inventive design, as this private view invite by Radley Yeldar, commissioned for Tate Britain, illustrates. Apparently sterile, a centred die cut offers a 'private view' of what lies inside the invite, namely a portrait by Lucian Freud.

Client: Rabih Hage
Design: Hat-trick
Process: Die-cut stationery
range on uncoated stock

Rabih Hage

Hat-trick used the natural relationship between the letters 'r' and 'h' for stationery for interior design company Rabih Hage. The 'r' is die cut out of the 'h', which is printed on all items to represent the initials of Rabih Hage and provide a window to the interior content, creating consistency with the company's business – interiors. Shown here is a folded business card from the range.

Reveals and discovery

Using reveals, or 'punch-throughs' allows a sense of discovery on the part of the user. This controlling of pace and content can help to form stories, narratives and a sense of journey. It can also add a sense of interactivity and order, with certain 'parts' of the information being released at staged intervals.

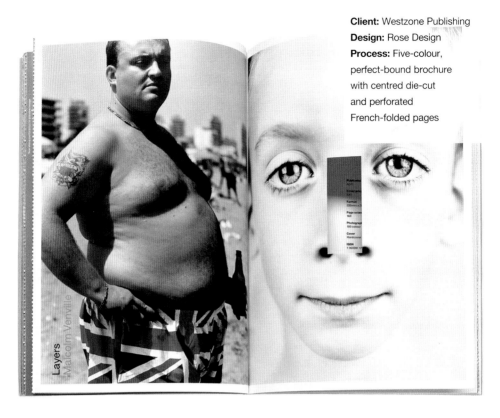

Client: Westzone Publishing

Design: Rose Design

Process: Five-colour, perfect-bound brochure with centred die-cut and perforated French-folded pages

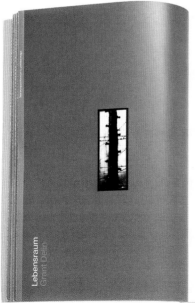

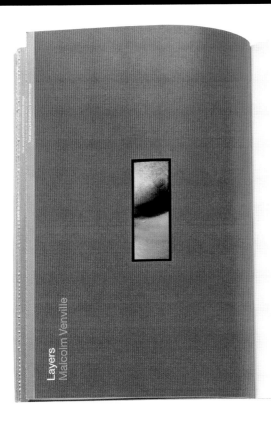

Publication
April

Cover price
£30

Format
320mm x 285mm

Page extent
160

Photography
400 colour

Cover
Hardcover

ISBN
1 903391 17 2

Title
A hearing child born to profoundly deaf parents, Malcolm Venville's formative years were spent in a world dominated by signs and gestures. The fact that Venville became a photographer is a direct extension of that early silent world which was purely visual.

This collection of images is also a lucid guide to the reality of taking photographs, not only in a technical sense but also in an emotional sense. Layers compiles images from famous advertising campaigns alongside Venville's own explorations in portraiture and the nude.

It pulls back the curtains and exposes what takes place immediately before and after a photograph is taken, from the banal technical facts regarding details such as formats and printing to the histories of the subjects in front of the lens.

Author
Malcolm Venville is a major figure on the British photography scene. He has photographed and directed advertising campaigns for Adidas, Gordon's Gin, The Millennium Commission, and has shot works for Nike, Mercury, Volkswagen and Guinness.

Westzone Publishing

Rose Design created this catalogue for Westzone Publishing, a company based in Venice, Italy as part of an identity to put the company firmly on the publishing map. Pictured is the preview catalogue of its titles with a die-cut aperture that enables the reader to see through to subsequent pages. This creates a juxtaposition of images, from the harrowing views of Auschwitz to the reportage photography of Malcom Venville. The French-folded pages are perforated on the outer edge, enabling readers to open them and discover the full 'story' the image has to tell.

Storytelling | **Form follows function** | Industry view: Mercy

Macedonian Museum
of Contemporary Art

This subtle exhibition catalogue takes readers on a journey of discovery. Hidden within the flaps of the book cover lies a fold-out image which sits in stark contrast to the book's delicate monochrome tonality, unexpectedly displaying a rush of colour but also a strange sense of calm due to the image portrayed (pages 30–31).

Marina Abramovic
Pietà, 2002
courtesy Lia Rumma, Naples

Client: Macedonian Museum
of Contemporary Art
Design: The Design Shop
Process: Use of fold-out
cover flaps for image
presentation

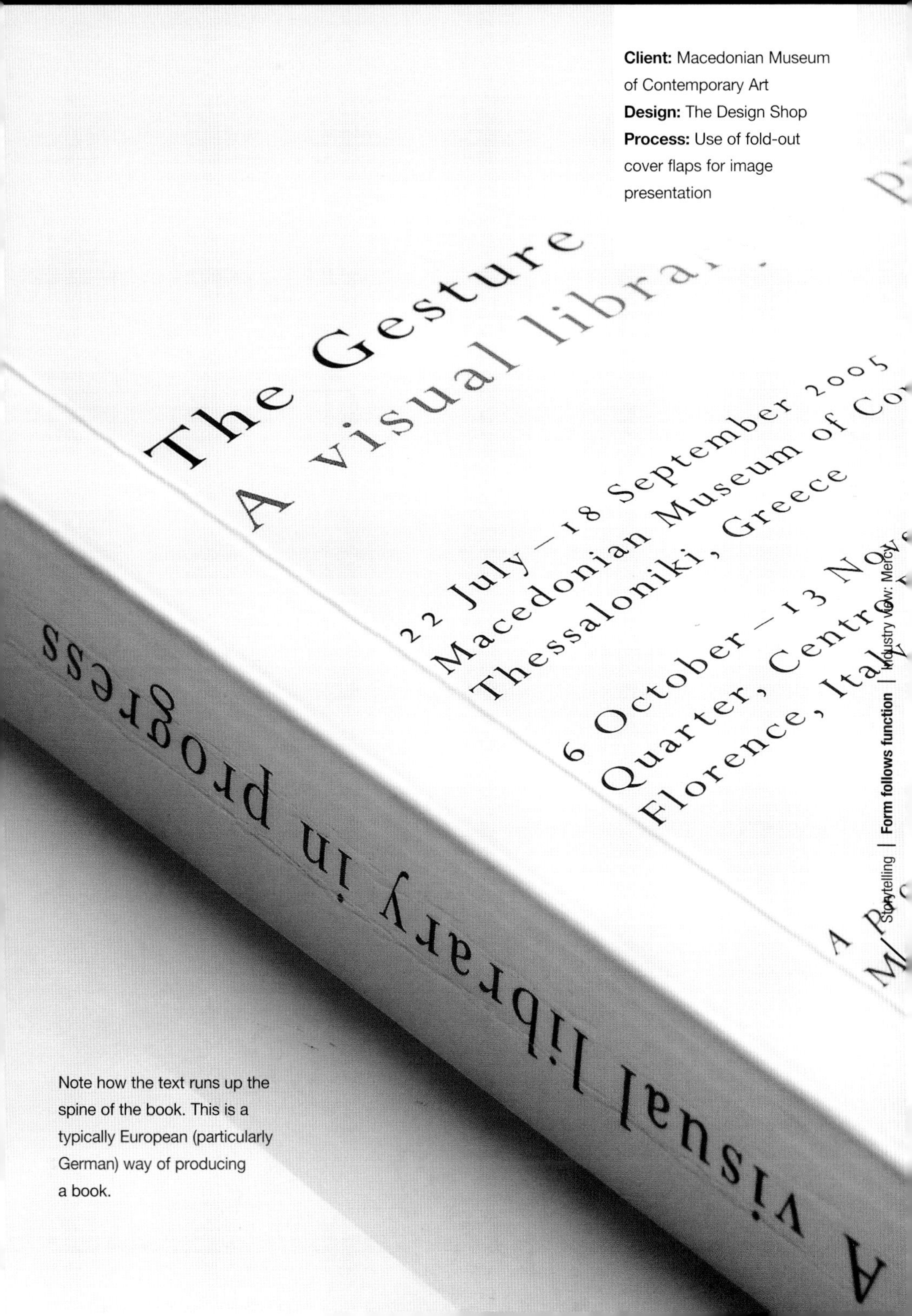

The Gesture

A visual libra.

22 July — 18 September 2005
Macedonian Museum of Co
Thessaloniki, Greece

6 October — 13 No
Quarter, Centr
Florence, Ital

A visual library in progress

Note how the text runs up the
spine of the book. This is a
typically European (particularly
German) way of producing
a book.

Client: Capital Commitment
Design: Hat-trick design
Process: Four-colour litho,
foil-blocked covers, embossed
box with spot varnish

Capital Commitment

With the marketing of real estate, taking ownership of an address has distinct
advantages. Potential buyers begin to see a building as an important part of an
already important street, and this sales brochure for a new building at 30 Gresham
Street, London, designed by Hat-trick design, does just that – by employing the
use of the number 30 throughout. The lid has 30 words representing the values of
the development embossed on it, and the box contains two half-sized brochures
with '30' foil-blocked on the covers. One brochure contains 30 words and the other
contains 30 accompanying images. A series of guides of the neighbouring vicinity
covers '30 points of view', '30 minutes around Gresham Street', '30 illustrious
neighbours' and a map with '30 ways to Gresham Street'.

Client: Delta Air Lines
Design: Turnbull Ripley
Process: Four-colour litho
with polypropylene case

Delta Air Lines

Rather than producing a single publication covering all elements of the sales kit for Delta Air Lines, Turnbull Ripley broke down the various components of the kit into separate publications for product offerings, bonuses and the different travel classes. This method divides (sometimes complex) information into easily managed blocks.

Order / randomness

Designers often want to control the order in which information is disseminated. However, there is a value in not trying to control or prescribe this, and in simply letting users 'experience' or create a narrative for themselves instead.

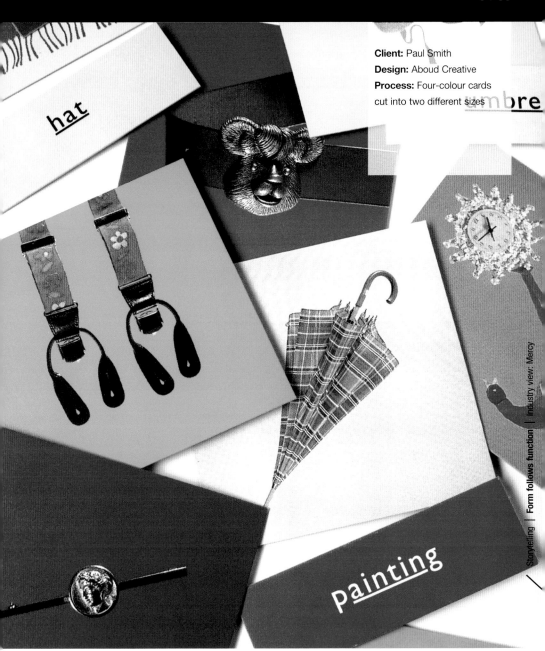

tie s

tea pot

hat

Client: Paul Smith
Design: Aboud Creative
Process: Four-colour cards cut into two different sizes

painting

Storytelling | **Form follows function** | Industry view: Mercy

Paul Smith

This catalogue for British fashion designer Paul Smith is based on a children's card game in which objects are matched with their names. A series of cards featuring products and associated name plaques offer a playful randomness to the order.

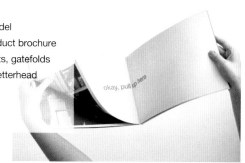

Client: Doric
Design: Roundel
Process: Product brochure
with throw-outs, gatefolds
and inserted letterhead

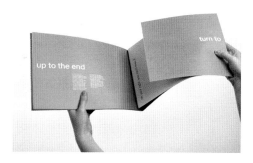

Doric

Entitled 'turn to', this poster/brochure
uses written instructions to instruct
readers how to unfold the product.
Completion of each instruction reveals
another page, gatefold or throw-up.

CTD CAPITA DIGITAL
INDICHROME™ SYSTEM
INTRODUCTION

CTD CAPITA DIGITAL
DIGITAL

HERRING

BERRY

CTD
CTD CAPITA DIGITAL

TEA

CTD CAPITA DIGITAL

WIDOW

CTD CAPITA DIGITAL

Client: CTD Capita Digital
Design: Hat-trick
Process: Printed one side only, bound by a bolt, with a laminated cover

CTD Capita Digital

This design for a guide to the new Indichrome printing system is based on the Pantone colour swatch book and produces more accurate colours than previous digital printing services, highlighted in the design by printing the 'names' of various colour hues and intensities in their respective colours.

Storytelling | **Form follows function** | Industry view: Mercy

Client: Issey Miyake
Design: Research Studios
Process: Four-colour, die-cut
brochure with loose-leaf insert

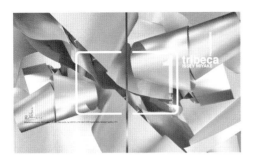

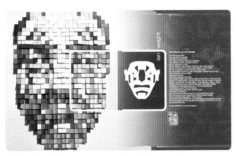

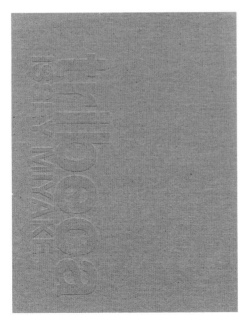

Issey Miyake

Research Studios used a subtle but effective die cut for this brochure for the Issey Miyake store in Tribeca, New York. Artists, musicians and designers were commissioned to show pieces alongside the branded goods within the store, and this juxtaposition is maintained in the brochure's design; this has a central die cut that forms two 'U' shapes either side of the spine (the silver brackets in the middle of the spreads). These provide a physical separation by creating a small book within the pages of the larger one so that readers can flip through either section independently. The work was protected by an embossed outer sleeve (shown left).

Industry view: Mercy

How do you come to choose the right format for a given design project? And how do you create a unique piece of design using a traditional format? In the following interview, Doug Kerr of Mercy design studio discusses his thought processes behind employing the familiarity of the postcard format to send an informal, friendly mailer to existing and prospective clients.

These promotional cards are of a standard postcard size, to which there is a distinct familiarity. Was it an intentional choice to use a size that people are familiar with?
We knew that we would be sending them out as direct mail, so the traditional postcard format seemed perfectly fitting. The added bonus lies in that by creating a traditional postcard, the recipient may choose to actually use it as a postcard, so it then goes onto someone else and we get a further hit of promotion.

More generally, we have a lot of clients that dictate the format of a job and we just go along with that. When we do have free rein, then we will research different formats and try and successfully convince a client to do something unusual (we recently attempted to convince someone to ditch a print job in favour of a purely audio solution, for instance).

You chose to deliver these cards in a traditional printed format, but they could equally have been sent digitally. Did you consider this?
We regularly produce online-only content, the most notable example being the 12-issue e-zine project that we released on our website over the course of 2010. At the moment, we are in the process of devising about four or five self-directed digital and digital/print crossover projects that will materialize over the coming 18 months. But we still think that nothing beats getting a handwritten envelope through the letterbox with a nice bit of print inside. And when it comes to a piece of direct mail such as this, we think that the immediacy of that experience makes a far bigger impact than something you simply receive in your email inbox.

Opposite: an example of one of the cards sent in the promotional pack

A RAINY DAY
IS THE PERFECT TIME
FOR A WALK IN THE WOODS,
WHERE IDEAS
CAN NO MORE
FLOW BACKWARDS
THAN A RIVER

Rachel Carson
Victor Hugo —

How does a choice of format either add to or detract from a message?

It's all about knowing your audience and your message I guess. For this project, our goal was a 'call to arms' – we wanted people to get something from us, then feel compelled to find out more. I think that if we'd uploaded a jpeg and then emailed it, it would have been too disposable. Instead, we went to the trouble of screenprinting them, packaging them up nicely in coloured paper with a little message, and handwriting the envelopes. It's a little thing, but I think it goes that extra mile – and the process of receiving it makes the recipient stop for a few moments and think about us.

How does the studio approach different formats? Do you look to be different or is it more about being appropriate to a certain message?

As well as working as an agency, we are lucky enough to have Arts Council backing, with which we run an entirely self-directed arts programme. When producing design work for that, we like to push ourselves to try out new and different formats, as we only have ourselves and our audience to think about – and they tend to be quite willing to be challenged. The great thing about this is that we then find it easier to run new formats by clients, as we'll have tried and tested examples in the portfolio already.

Mercy produce cutting-edge graphic design and illustration for a range of clients as diverse as major record labels, international property developers, fashion labels and architects. Mercy's client roster includes big names such as Universal, Sony, Diesel and Virgin. **www.mercyonline.co.uk**

Design activity:
Messages and formats

Premise
The choices offered by format can be varied and exciting. But underpinning these decisions lies a common desire – the conveyance of information. Ultimately, a designer is trying to convey a message. To do this effectively, you need to understand both what you are trying to convey, and why you need to do this.

Exercise
1 Take the format of a postage stamp (10–30mm x 10–30mm or 0.4–1.2 in x 0.4–1.2 in), a postcard (88.9–108mm x 127–152.4mm or 3.5–4.3in x 5.0–6.0in) and an A1 poster (594mm x 841mm or 23.4in x 33.1 in).

2 Explore how a series of messages can be conveyed through the use of typography or image. Your objective is to encourage people to: use a library; reduce their sugar and salt intake; vote for a particular political party; or to take more exercise.

3 Produce a series of typographical or image-based responses to these issues, presented on both formats.

Aim
This project is about reducing a complex issue to an understandable amount of information. Just because the poster offers more space than a stamp doesn't necessarily mean that you have to use more text! Artists like Shepard Fairey, Jenny Holzer and Banksy demonstrate how the reduction of information, often to a short epigram, can be powerful. Shepard Fairey's poster for Barack Obama's election campaign relied on a single word, 'hope'.

Outcome
You will understand how messages are distilled and conveyed in relation to scale.

Suggested reading
- *Mayday: The Art of Shepard Fairey* by Jeffrey Deitch (Gingko Press, 2010)
- *Wall and Piece* by Banksy (Random House, 2005)
- *Off the Wall: Political Posters of the Lebanese Civil War* by Zeina Maasri (I.B. Tauris, 2008)
- *Revolutionary Tides: The Art of the Political Poster 1914-1989* by Jeffrey T. Schnapp (Skira, 2005)
- *Jenny Holzer (Contemporary Artists)* by Jenny Holzer (Phaidon Press, 1998)

Client: D&AD
Design: Frost Design
Process: Single-colour print
on newsprint. Endorse folded

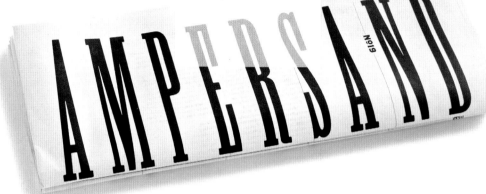

Covering 'fiction, pictures, poetry, pop'
The Illustrated Ape certainly knows where to
draw the line, says Liz Hancock

MONKEY
BUSINESS

The InnoTown conference in Norway attracts the
crème de la crème in design innovation, but they're
not the main attraction for Henrietta Thompson

INNOVATIONS
CATALOGUE

Chapter 2
Printed media

Some of the most important parts of history have been marked by the production of printed matter. From the Magna Carta, the Book of Kells and The Declaration of Independence, through to the political propaganda posters of the 20th century, printed matter is of unrivalled importance and stature.

Alongside these works of national and international importance, our cultural make-up is also constructed by the printed ephemera that surrounds us. Some printed items are intended to be kept as a record, as a cultural marker in time. There is also a plethora of printed items that are transitory and temporary in nature.

This section looks at the many outputs of printed media, from the book through to brochures and posters. The choice of format here is varied and often unconventional – with designers challenging the norms and conventions of any given media.

'Societies have always been shaped more by the nature of the media by which men communicate than by the content of the communication.'

Marshall McLuhan

Purpose and narrative | **Printed media** | Construction

D&AD

This design by Frost Design for a D&AD newsletter borrows heavily from newspapers in terms of its format, scale, design and typography, which includes Jim-dashes (short rules dividing information), kickers (lines of copy appearing above or below an article), necklines (white spaces under running heads), standfirsts (introductory paragraphs), and mastheads (titles and visual keystones of a publication). The use of this format lends the presented information a currency and authority that compels people to read it. The newspaper effect is finished with an 'endorse' fold. This is where the printed item is folded (usually in half) after binding.

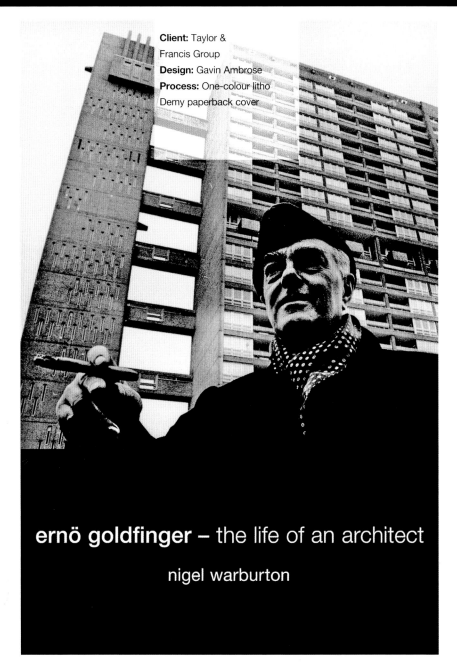

Client: Taylor & Francis Group
Design: Gavin Ambrose
Process: One-colour litho
Demy paperback cover

ernö goldfinger – the life of an architect

nigel warburton

Taylor & Francis Group
Peter Hamilton photographed the architect Ernö Goldfinger in front of Trellick Tower in west London, which he designed, for this Demy book cover.

Book formats

Two main factors affect the final size of a book: the size of the original sheet of paper, and the number of times the sheet of paper is folded before trimming. Shown below are the common sizes of books, both modern and traditional.

Modern book formats	Imperial (inches approx.)	Metric (mm)
Demy	9 x 6	229 x 152
Royal	9 1/4 x 7 1/2	235 x 191
Crown Royal	11 x 8 1/4	280 x 210
Classic hardback or C format paperback	8 3/4 x 5 5/8	222 x 143
'Trade' paperback or B format	8 x 5 1/4	198 x 129

Traditional book formats	Imperial (inches approx.)	Metric (mm)
Imperial folio	15 ½ x 22	390 x 550
Royal folio	12 ½ x 20	320 x 500
Imperial quarto	11 x 15	280 x 300
Crown folio	10 x 15	250 x 300
Royal quarto	10 x 12 ½	250 x 320
Medium quarto	9 ½ x 12	240 x 300
Demy quarto	8 ¾ x 11 ¼	220 x 290
Foolscap folio	8 ½ x 13 ½	210 x 340
Imperial octavo	7 ½ x 11	190 x 280
Crown quarto	7 ½ x 10	190 x 250
Foolscap quarto	6 ¾ x 8 ½	170 x 210
Royal octavo	6 ¼ x 10	150 x 250
Medium octavo	6 x 9 ½	150 x 240
Demy octavo (demy 8vo)	5 5/8 x 8 ¾	143 x 222
Large crown octavo	5 ¼ x 8	129 x 198
Crown octavo	5 x 7 ½	127 x 190
Foolscap octavo	4 ¼ x 6 ¾	108 x 171.5
'A' format 'Pulp fiction'	4 ¼ x 6 7/8	111 x 175

Book formats | Imposition and multiple stocks

Client: Levi's® RED™
Design: The Kitchen
Process: Look book in the
form of a sculptural book

Levi's® RED™

Each fashion season throws up different themes that need to be worked into the designs that promote the clothing. The theme for this press brochure for Levi's® RED™ was glass. The Kitchen therefore used die-cut pages to reduce the photography of Tim Bret-Day to shards, creating an unusual piece that sits in harmony with the season's theme.

Corbis (page 49)

The removal of stock via a die cut opens up a host of visual possibilities in a design. In this example for a Corbis product licensing catalogue entitled 'Sample', the cover is die cut with the shapes of several common objects. Laying this over the images within the catalogue shows what an image would look like as a sofa, a vase, a cup and so on, opening up new avenues for image experimentation by the stock photography purchaser.

Client: Corbis
Design: Segura Inc.
Process: Four-colour litho book with die-cut cover

Book formats | imposition and multiple stocks

Client: Nigel Coates/
Laurence King Publishing
Design: why not associates
Process: 408-page book,
edition bound, multiple
page-markers, foil-blocked
cover and bellyband

Nigel Coates/Laurence King Publishing

why not associates made a useful enhancement to
the format of architect Nigel Coates' book *Ecstacity*
by including several coloured page marker bands. The
markers highlight the complex dynamics and multiple
narratives that characterize today's urban metropolis,
which are the focus of this book.

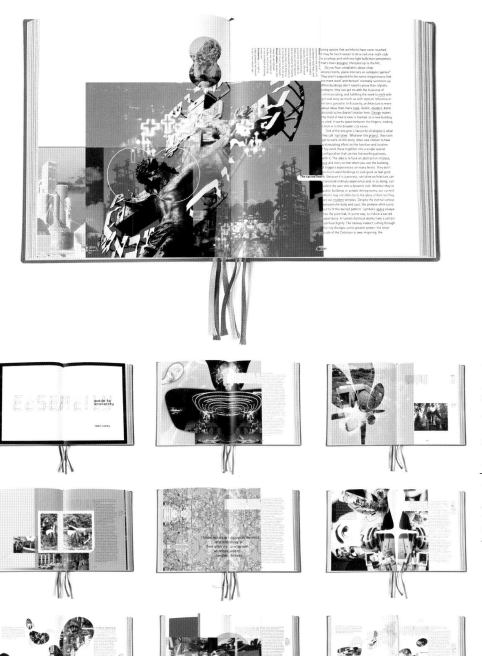

Imposition and multiple stocks

With a simple four-colour job, imposition is not important as every page prints with the same four process colours. If you have the budget or the chance to alter the colour fall, however, such as by using a special colour or spot varnish, more intricate planning may be necessary. You will need to know which pages will need to carry the spot colour by means of an imposition plan.

An imposition plan provides an economic benefit by reducing the number of sections that you need to print with the special colour. This plan also allows you to maximize the coverage of a special colour; for example, pages 82, 83, 86, 87, 90, 91, 94 and 95 of this book all print with an additional fifth colour, Pantone 877 metallic. On an imposition plan, these would all fall on the same side of one 16-page section, as shown opposite.

Having a pagination plan can help simplify colour-fall and allows you to see other pages that can benefit from the addition of an additional colour or special treatment.

Any additional print finishing techniques are also included in this plan, for example gatefolds, throwouts and any tip-ins.

This book prints to the imposition plan shown below. As it's bound in 16-page sections, there are eight pages to view (that is, eight pages on each side of the sheet). It is specified as a 208-page book with a six-panel gatefold, containing an eight-page uncoated section at the back.

1	2	3	4	5	6	7	8	9	10	11	12	13	14	15	16
17	18	19	20	21	22	23	24	25	26	27	28	29	30	31	32
33	34	35	36	37	38	39	40	41	42	43	44	45	46	47	48
49	50	51	52	53	54	55	56	57	58	59	60	61	62	63	64

Four four-colour
16-page sections.

If you open a book, page 1 obviously backs-up with page 2, page 3 with 4, page 5 with 6 and so on. When specifying colour fall, remember this and it should be straightforward. In the first 16-page section above, pages 1, 4, 5, 8, 9, 12, 13 and 16 print together, with the remaining pages printing on the reverse. This means that these two groups of eight pages can be treated separately, as shown in section six below, printed in a special colour.

64a	64b	64c
64d	64e	64f

Tip-ins are normally spliced between sections.
This six-panel tip-in falls between pages 64 and 65.
It could, however, fall between any of the sections
in this book.

Six-panel tip-in.

65	66	67	68	69	70	71	72	73	74	75	76	77	78	79	80
81	82	83	84	85	86	87	88	89	90	91	92	93	94	95	96
97	98	99	100	101	102	103	104	105	106	107	108	109	110	111	112
113	114	115	116	117	118	119	120	121	122	123	124	125	126	127	128
129	130	131	132	133	134	135	136	137	138	139	140	141	142	143	144
145	146	147	148	149	150	151	152	153	154	155	156	157	158	159	160
161	162	163	164	165	166	167	168	169	170	171	172	173	174	175	176
177	178	179	180	181	182	183	184	185	186	187	188	189	190	191	192
193	194	195	196	197	198	199	200								
201	202	203	204	205	206	207	208								

Eight four-colour
16-page sections.

A special colour has been applied to the highlighted pages in the ninth section. As the sections are printed eight-to-view, these all fall on one side of a section.

8 pages are then printed separately – to make 200 pages, with a final single-colour eight-page section printed on woodfree paper.

Book formats | **Imposition and multiple stocks** | Scale

Client: Thomas Dunne Books
Design: Rose Design
Process: Book with uncoated and silk stocks, printed single-colour throughout and perfect-bound

Book formats | Imposition and multiple stocks | Scale

Thomas Dunne Books

For a book about The Beatles, Rose Design divided two distinct types of
information by using different stocks. A brown-coloured, uncoated stock carries
archival photography and the main text sections. A plain silk stock carries a series
of large quotes and non-archival photography by Sandro Sodano. The two stocks
enhance the contrast between the high quality of Sodano's studio photography
andthe mixed quality of the archival images. The book is formed of 14 eight-page,
four-colour sections on silk stock; and 11 eight-page, two-colour sections on
uncoated stock that are printed and spliced to create the mixed pagination.

LIVERPOOL JOHN MOORES UNIVERSITY
LEARNING SERVICES

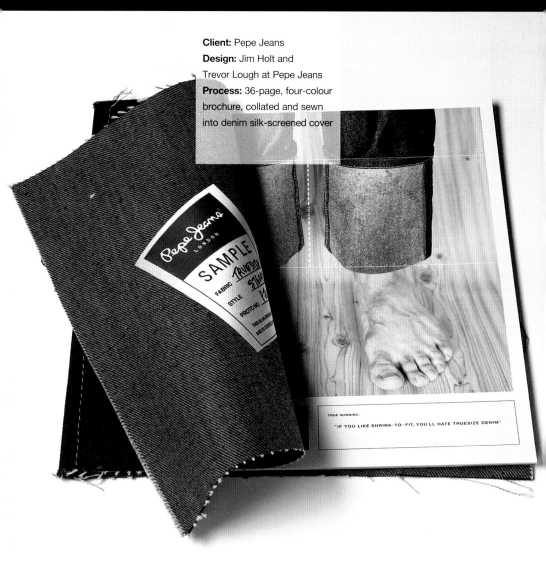

Client: Pepe Jeans
Design: Jim Holt and
Trevor Lough at Pepe Jeans
Process: 36-page, four-colour
brochure, collated and sewn
into denim silk-screened cover

TRUE WARNING:
"IF YOU LIKE SHRINK-TO-FIT, YOU'LL HATE TRUESIZE DENIM"

Pepe Jeans

Jim Holt and Trevor Lough stuck as close to the theme as possible for this brochure
for Pepe Jeans – by basing the design around a pair of jeans. The cover substrate
is denim cloth, on the inside of which is the information usually found on a book's
front cover, on a label made from the same material as that of Pepe jeans.

NESTA

For the cover of a brochure for NESTA – the UK's National Endowment for Science, Technology and the Arts – Hat-trick design used a self-adhesive substrate kiss cut into stickers, inviting readers to distribute the 'subject to change' message they carry.

Client: NESTA
Design: Hat-trick
Process: Saddle-stitched brochure with single-colour, self-adhesive kiss-cut cover

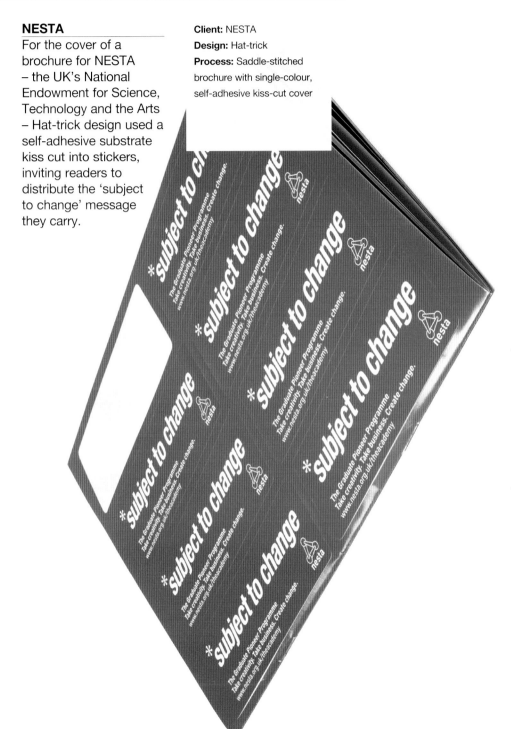

Book formats | **Imposition and multiple stocks** | Scale

Client: Focus Gallery
Design: MadeThought
Process: Wrap-cover
brochures with three
different bellybands

Bellyband

A bellyband is a paper or plastic substrate that wraps around the 'belly' of a publication. The substrate may be a full loop or a strip. Commonly used on magazines, they serve to produce an eye-catching piece of information.

Focus Gallery

For this catalogue for a Bill Brandt exhibition at the Focus Gallery in London, MadeThought specified that the central pages should be cut with a shorter width than the multi-panel wrap-cover enclosing it. The front cover folds out so that readers can see information about works in the exhibition as they browse the content pages. The exhibition catalogue was produced with three different bellybands featuring key images from the show.

Plate No.17 / One Gun Street, refuge building cast facade.

Fig. 28

Tip-ins

A tip-in is a means to attach an insert into a book or magazine by gluing along the binding edge.

It is a method for attaching individual elements into a publication, such as colour plates, that are typically produced on a different stock where insufficient pages are required to warrant printing a separate section.

Client: Manhattan
Loft Corporation
Design: North
Process: Six-colour
brochure using various
stocks tipped-in to
main body

Manhattan Loft Corporation
North used seven stocks to produce a mélange of textures for this brochure
celebrating ten years of property developer Manhattan Loft Corporation.
Colour plates set in white frames contain commissioned photography of the area.
The frames are separated by translucent tip-ins, while undersized tip-ins of a
heavier stock are used to provide additional reference information and atmospheric
imagery. All the tip-ins bind from the same edge of the book (the bottom in this
case) – a usual requirement when collating and binding.

Scale

Scale can have a dramatic effect on a design, making an item instantly more interesting. Making an intentional choice through scale can make a tangible point of difference, marking your design out from the crowd. Many contemporary designers have exploited and explored the use of scale.

Irma Boom, the prominent Dutch book designer, famously produced a 2136-page book called *SHV Think Book 1996–1896,* which has become an icon of modern Dutch design. In contrast, she has also developed a series of 'fat books'. These miniature books, around two inches tall, were originally used as maquettes or mock-ups for other projects, but are now produced as books in their own right.

FI@33

For a publication containing images of cranes on the skyline, FI@33 chose an oversized, loose-leaf magazine format. The format selection marries with the oversized scale of the machinery depicted in the photographs.

Maquette
(French for scale model) a maquette is a small draft or model of a larger work. Making a small 'dummy' of a book allows a designer to see the flow of images and spread of colour without having the distraction of readable text.

Client: Self-initiated project
by Fl@33
Design: Fl@33
Process: Four-colour litho
oversized loose-leaf journal

Imposition and multiple stocks | **Scale** | Throw-outs and gatefolds

Client: Gagosian Gallery
Design: Bruce Mau Design
Process: Four-colour folded brochure/poster that measures over 1.5m x 1m when opened, with perforated guides

Richard Hamilton: Products™

Gagosian Gallery

Bruce Mau Design created this poster for an exhibition by pop artist Richard Hamilton at the Gagosian Gallery in London. It is a 32-panel fold-down poster that has perforated edges to help it fold. The large-format poster opens to reveal a near life-size image by Rita Donagh of the artist carrying one of his works, 'Epiphany', produced in 1964.

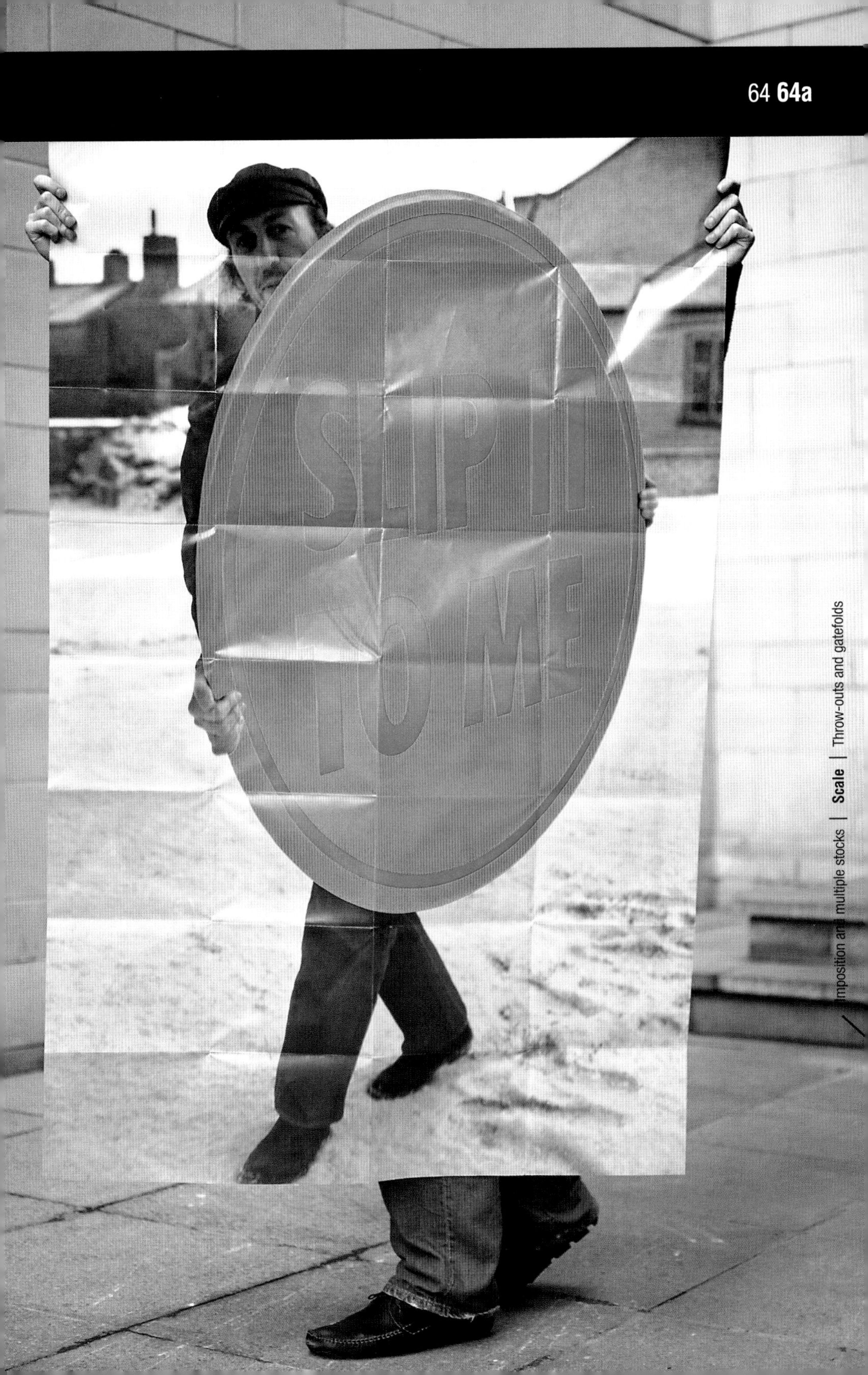
SLIP IT
TO ME

ISSN 1322-5901

PREMIERE ISSUE, BI-ANNUAL AUTUMN/WINTER 2001 UK£ 4.99

ANOTHER GAZINE

FOR MEN AND WOMEN

Client: Another Magazine
Design: Art direction by
Stella McCartney
Process: Four-panel gatefold
printed in four colours,
tipped-in to perfect binding

Gatefold

A gatefold has extra panels that fold into the central spine of the publication with parallel folds so that they meet in the middle of the page. The extended pages are folded and cut shorter than the standard publication pages so that they can nest correctly. Gatefolds are commonly used in magazines.

Throw-outs and throw-ups

Throw-outs and throw-ups are sheets of paper folded into a publication. They can be used to showcase a particular image, example or other visual element by allowing a larger scale to be used, and better printability if a better stock is used. This gatefold contains a throw-out for 'Another Magazine' that was art directed by fashion designer Stella McCartney. An example of a throw-up can be seen on page 64f.

Client: Levi's®
Design: The Kitchen
Process: Four-colour litho with tipped-in throw-ups

Levi's®

Jeans manufacturer Levi's® entitled its Denim Delinquent book *"no"* in homage to the writer Albert Camus, who wrote, 'What is a rebel? A man who says "no"'. To emphasize the rebellion angle, The Kitchen staged its own formatting rebellion in the design. Spliced between the pages of the book are nine four-colour throw-ups with a French fold, featuring images of rockers, tomboys and other rebellious types to add anti-authoritarian chic to the clothing line. The book cover is cloth-bound with embossed lettering.

Throw-ups

A throw-up is a substrate that is folded into a publication, typically with larger dimensions than the work that contains it, and possibly of a different stock, and is designed to showcase a particular image.

Client: Plantology
Design: Iris Associates
Process: Five posters
(210mm x 430mm) folded
into six panels, glued together
and contained between
two foil-blocked boards

Plantology

Iris Associates designed a series of five posters, or throw-ups, that were folded into six panels for a brochure for client Plantology, a florist. The throw-ups (with one horizontal and two vertical folds) fold out to show striking flower photography. The folded posters are glued between heavyweight foil-blocked boards.

Magazines

The magazine has become an artistic expression of ideas and form. Narrative is often dominated by images and the sequence that they are presented in. The magazine format offers a lot of scope for creative experimentation.

Tank

Pioneering magazine *Tank* takes many forms – be it playing with scale and form, or pushing the boundaries of content. Shown right is an issue called *365 days later*, which was printed at an unusually small size. Shown (far right) is a special edition available without images, and the corresponding mainstream issue that came complete with images.

Client: *Tank*

Design: Tank

Process: Various issues in different formats ranging from the 350mm x 280mm oversized to the 70mm x 55mm miniature version

FROM

LOD Z

TO

WAR SAW

Client: *Code* magazine
Design: Toko
Process: Magazine using a variety of grids, typefaces and page layouts to create a sense of pace and dynamism

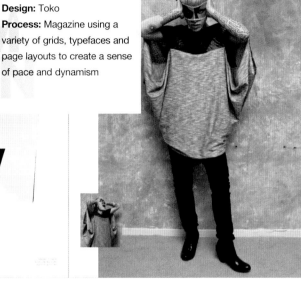

Code magazine

Toko's design work for *Code* magazine dates back nearly a decade, when they first designed the masthead and initial issue. Subsequent issues have used a variety of different layouts, bespoke typefaces and special sections of editorial content. *Code* reports on style and fashion through the use of 'real' people, giving the publication a point of difference in the style magazine department. The avant-garde and sometimes reportage approach taken has led to *Code* becoming a platform for emerging designers and brands.

Posters

Posters surround us – on billboards, buses and taxis, they are endemic to the urban environment. Shown are the common standard and large poster sizes.

Posters are divided into two main categories. Those that are relatively small in format are, in Europe, taken from the ISO A series (a series of sizes from postcard and writing sizes, through to small poster sizes). Paper sizes are as shown below:

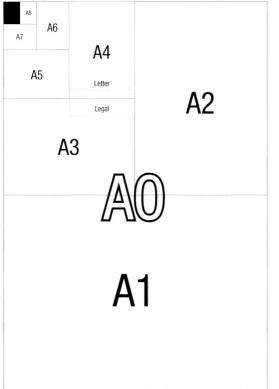

A series paper sizes H x W

(shown in mm and then inches as this series is based upon a metric measurement)

4A0	2378 x 1682 mm	93.6 x 66.2 in
2A0	1682 x 1189 mm	66.2 x 46.8 in
A0	1189 x 841 mm	46.8 x 33.1 in
A1	841 x 594 mm	33.1 x 23.4 in
A2	594 x 420 mm	23.4 x 16.5 in
A3	420 x 297 mm	16.5 x 11.7 in
A4	297 x 210 mm	11.7 x 8.3 in
A5	210 x 148.5 mm	8.3 x 5.8 in
A6	148.5 x 105 mm	5.8 x 4.1 in
A7	105 x 74 mm	4.1 x. 2.9 in
A8	74 x 52 mm	2.9 x 2.0 in
A9	52 x 37 mm	2.0 x 1.5 in
A10	37 x 26 mm	1.5 x 1.0 in

US paper sizes H x W

(shown in mm and then inches as this series is based upon a metric measurement)

Letter	216 x 279 mm	8.5 x 11 in
Legal	216 x 356 mm	8.5 x 14 in
Ledger	279 x 432 mm	11 x 17 in
Super A3	330 x 483 mm	13 x 19 in

Larger, outdoor media sizes are based around a system called sheets, with the basic building block being a 4 sheet, that is 60 x 40 inches in size. By adding sheets, larger sizes can be made, for example, a 12 sheet is three 4 sheets, placed side-by-side. In all instances, the sheets are placed making a horizontal poster format, with the exception of the 16 sheet (4 x 4 posters) which is used to create a vertical format.

4 sheet

12 sheet

16 sheet

32 sheet

Magazines | **Posters** | Industry view: Andy Vella

Outdoor media sizes

(shown in inches and then mm as this series is based upon imperial measurement)

4-sheet poster	60in x 40in	1016mm x 1524mm
12-sheet poster	120in x 60in	3048mm x 1524mm
16-sheet poster	80in x 120in	2036mm x 3048mm
32-sheet poster	160in x 120in	4064mm x 3048mm
48-sheet poster	240in x 120in	6096mm x 3048mm
64-sheet poster	320in x 120in	8128mm x 3048mm
96-sheet poster	480in x 120in	12192mm x 3048mm

The only size that doesn't adhere to this convention is the six-sheet poster, which is a bespoke size used primarily for bus-stop advertising. This is a single sheet of 1200mm x 1800mm.

Client: Association of
Valencian designers
Design: Lavernia &
Cienfuegos Diseño
Process: Lithographic poster
exploring typography and the
division of space

Association of Valencian designers

This poster for an exhibition of typography uses standard paper sizes as a means of exploring the relationships between different type sizes and weights. The perimeter of the poster becomes as important as the central print area.

Client: *Creative Review*
Design: Pentagram
(Angus Hyland)
Process: Four-colour litho
with perforations

Magazines | **Posters** | Industry view: Andy Vella

Creative Review

This poster for *Creative Review* magazine was designed by Angus Hyland at Pentagram to promote a student subscription offer. It invited people to deconstruct the poster and to create something new with it. The poster is made up of a double sheet, with a fold along the top edge separating the top 'TEAR ME UP' from the bottom sheet. Each letter is perforated through the middle, providing an element of interaction, so that as they are removed, details of the subscription are revealed.

Ravensbourne College of Design and Communication

Rather than create a publication with a spine for the prospectus for Ravensbourne College of Design and Communication in the UK, MadeThought created a folded poster wrap that opens to reveal a student hard at work. This is in stark contrast to the majority of prospectuses that normally have a similar format to this book. The format used also allows the information to be arranged according to the folded panels, bringing a hierarchical order to the piece.

Poster wraps

A poster wrap is used to form a loose, informal cover for a publication that can be removed and opened out to reveal a poster format, so combining the practicalities of a dust jacket with the scale and effect of the poster.

Client: Ravensbourne College
of Design and Communication
Design: MadeThought
Process: Four-colour
fold-down poster/prospectus

Industry view: Andy Vella

As art director for publishing house Foruli, Andy Vella has pushed the boundaries of the 'book' format. His recent work for the Foruli title *Becoming Elektra* for the legendary Elektra Records label has resulted in the creation of lavishly and thoughtfully produced issues forming a collectable and engaging series of works, which demonstrate the creative possibilities that format and print techniques can offer.

The use of materials and textures plays an important role in your work. In the example opposite, fallen leather (leather from animals that die naturally), leatherette and even 1950s speaker cloth have been used. Do you actively try to push the boundaries of design and print manufacture?

For me, it is very important to push design in this way. I am really keen on using traditional methods of binding and taking them on a step further. What was great about this project was using craftsmen from The Fine Book Bindery (UK) and getting the best out of them. The way in which I would like to actually take a design may not always be possible – so consulting with craftsmen and finding a way to do it can involve compromise; as in this case, for example, using chunks of metal (blocks) to print with onto leather is a million miles away from seeing an idea on a wonderful backlit LCD, RGB-colour Mac screen.

Traditional letterpress knowledge has given me an understanding of using various different levels of pressure, which helps with embossing into a range of mediums.

Here, we have been able to create a very tactile object which seduces readers before they have even read the book. The 'E' for the Elektra logo uses the back/rough side of the leather which is then inlayed within the beautiful smooth side of the leather; the butterfly and logo are later blind embossed, and the type is white foil-blocked, so making use of both the good side and (often my favourite) bad or rough side of the object. The solander works as a total opposite; the fabrics, albeit 1950s, are synthetic and so push the contrasts between the subtle handmade, natural leather-bound embossed book nestling within the 1950s speaker box.

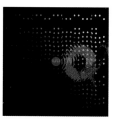

The nature of your work sees you interpreting music, and moving image into print. The choice of formats and printing techniques allows you to explore and engage with a reader. Can you elaborate on how this process works, with you as designer, and in many cases a musician as client?

With this die-cut house record sleeve for Foruli, I aimed to create a 3D object that works on various levels. It is a functioning piece of packaging which contains and protects the 10-inch vinyl and a limited-edition fine art print within. The design looks different within the sleeve as the holes only reveal certain parts of the image: on its own, the insert becomes another graphic, while other inserts within the house bag play with the spacing of the die-cut dots to create a moiré pattern.

The overall design uses a range of paper stocks. The bags are litho and gloss UV varnish, and the inserts are printed on a whole host of different mediums – usually screen-printed and sometimes on random screen fine-dot lithoprint, from black Mirri to silver Mirri board, to translucent and block board. These different textures relate to the music/artist that they are coupled with.

Above: a series of record covers produced for the Foruli house bag, featuring a series of die-cuts and experimental image representation.

Andy Vella is the owner of velladesign, which has produced design, photography and brand identities for a range of sectors for more than 25 years, notably the music business, advertising and book and magazine publishing. He also works as consultant art director for Foruli publications. His clients include Saatchi & Saatchi, XfM, Fiction Records, Universal, Planet Rock, Quercus Books and Penguin.
www.velladesign.com / www.foruli.co.uk

Design activity:
Breaking convention

Premise
Most printed items adhere to standard, conventional sizes and formats. There is a practical reason for this, and it also brings economic savings. But imagine if the everyday items we encounter weren't governed by these conventions?

Exercise
1 Take a piece of printed ephemera, be it a utility bill, book, invite or map.

2 Using a different set of 'conventional' formats, explore how the basic format choice allows you to reappropriate and reconfigure the information contained in the original item. For example, if you take the information contained in a utility bill that would normally be printed in A4 or US Letter format, then how would this be altered if afforded the space of a billboard poster?

3 Use one of the following suggested original items – a utility bill, recipe, music score or CD inlay. Then explore the information contained in the item using one of the following formats – book, poster, bus advertisement or protest banner.

Aim
To produce a series of experimental, deconstructed results.

Outcome
You will have started to discover how format has a fundamental influence on how we perceive information.

Suggested reading
- *Routledge Philosophy Guidebook to Derrida on Deconstruction (Routledge Philosophy Guidebooks)* by Barry Stocker (Routledge, 2006)
- *Experimental Formats: Books, Brochures and Catalogues (Pro-graphics)* by Chris Foges and Roger Fawcett-Tang (Rotovision, 2001)
- *Materials, Process, Print: Creative Solutions for Graphic Design* by Daniel Mason (Laurence King, 2007)
- *Print and Production Finishes for Brochures and Catalogs* by Roger Fawcett-Tang (Rockport Publishers, 2006)

Client: Sculpture at Goodwood
Design: MadeThought
Process: 48- and 176-page books connected by z-bind cover. Foil-blocked outer cover

Chapter 3
Construction

We often think of design as being a flat activity, with the results appearing on screen or on paper. By having an understanding of how paper can be manipulated, a sense of craft and engineering can be instilled into a design.

These innovative techniques can be used to add a sense of interest and uniqueness to a design, but they are also useful 'tools' for dissecting information and controlling pace. Designers use construction methods to compartmentalize information, as well as to order the way in which content is revealed.

'Craft is part of the creative process.'
Gavin Bryars

Sculpture at Goodwood

Z-binds are used in several of the projects in this book, but here is an interesting application by MadeThought for client Sculpture at Goodwood. The publication is entitled *Thinking Big, Concepts for Twenty-first Century British Sculpture*, with works from leading sculptors including Tony Cragg, Jon Buck and Andy Goldsworthy. The book comprises two parts: the front section contains detailed biographies of the sculptors that created the 85 works, while the back section contains atmospheric and abstract imagery by Richard Learoyd. The unique aspect of this design is that the two sections share a z-fold cover that both separates and unites the two halves.

Printed media | **Construction** | Identity and branding

Different types of fold

There are many unusual and interesting folding techniques available to add interest to a design.

Front / back accordion fold With three parallel folds, the two-panel outer wings fold into and out of the centre. The double panel centre serves as the cover.

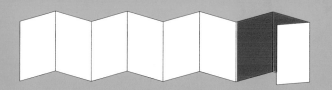

Mock book fold Essentially an accordion fold, where the penultimate two panels form a cover that the other panels then fold into to create a book.

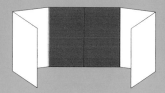 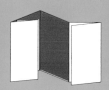

Front / back gatefold An extra double panel that folds inside the front and/or back panel.

Triple parallel fold Parallel folds that create a section that nests within the cover panels, with a front opening. May be used with maps.

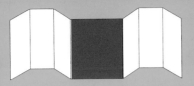

Back / front folder Wings either side of the central panel have a double parallel fold so that they can fold around and cover both sides of the central panel.

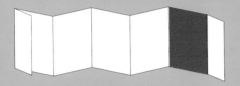

Half cover from behind An accordion fold where the penultimate panel forms a back cover that the other panels fold into to create a book, but the half-size end panel folds around the book from behind to cover the front together with the half-size first panel.

Duelling z-fold Z-fold wings fold into the centre panel and meet in the middle.

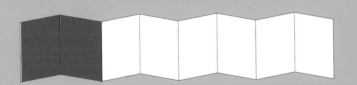

Harmonica self-cover folder An accordion fold where the first two panels form a cover that the other panels fold into. The first two panels need to be larger than the others to allow for creep.

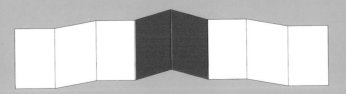

Double gatefold The gatefold has three panels that fold in towards the centre of the publication.

Different types of fold | Types of binding

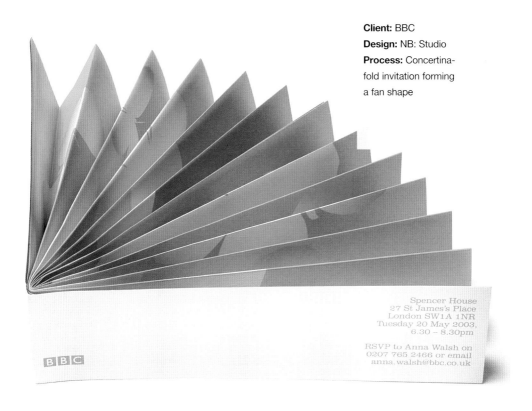

Client: BBC
Design: NB: Studio
Process: Concertina-
fold invitation forming
a fan shape

Spencer House
27 St James's Place
London SW1A 1NR
Tuesday 20 May 2003,
6.30 – 8.30pm

RSVP to Anna Walsh on
0207 765 2466 or email
anna.walsh@bbc.co.uk

B B C

BBC

This piece by NB: Studio for an invite to a 'BBC Radio & Music Summer Reception' perfectly illustrates the accordion fold (also known as a fan fold). Made from a single sheet of paper with accordion or concertina folds along its length and one right-angle fold to create a fan, a printed white substrate was then glued onto the outside. A combination of valley and mountain folds ensures that the fan retains its shape. The circular illusion of the fan is created by gluing the top two panels together.

Tate (page 85)

SEA Design chose to use a concertina fold in its design for a literature system for the UK's Tate galleries. A concertina fold is a folding method whereby each fold runs opposite to the previous one to obtain a pleated result. The fold physically divides up the area of the leaflet into equal manageable 'panels' on which the design can be organized.

Client: Tate
Design: SEA Design
Process: Concertina-fold
information updaters

The basic folds

There are essentially two basic folds that are used to construct even the most complex of printed items, the valley fold and the mountain fold. A valley fold is created when you fold the paper towards yourself: to make a mountain fold, you fold it behind or away from yourself. The two types of fold make basic mountain and valley shapes and form the basis of most folded pieces of design.

Valley fold   Mountain fold

Frost Design

With so many publications and documents in the A4 format, something rather different and more dramatic can be achieved with folding techniques. Folding adds to the physical texture of a piece and provides a novel way of dividing space or organizing the elements in the design, in effect creating a physical grid to guide it, as this example of Frost Design's portfolio shows.

Client: Frost Design
Design: Frost Design
Process: Concertina
litho-print, bonded to outer
board with foil-blocked type

Struktur

Struktur used a concertina fold to produce a self-promotional calendar that is almost three metres long when unfolded. The folding method here provides an obvious benefit as it enables the product to be condensed into a more manageable form and also provides physical pages upon which to position the design. The length of the calendar meant that it had to be printed in three sections that were fixed together; heavy embossed greyboard ends were then glued on to provide a protective carrier.

Client: Struktur
Design: Struktur
Process: 18-panel concertina fold, printed in three sections and bonded to a greyboard cover

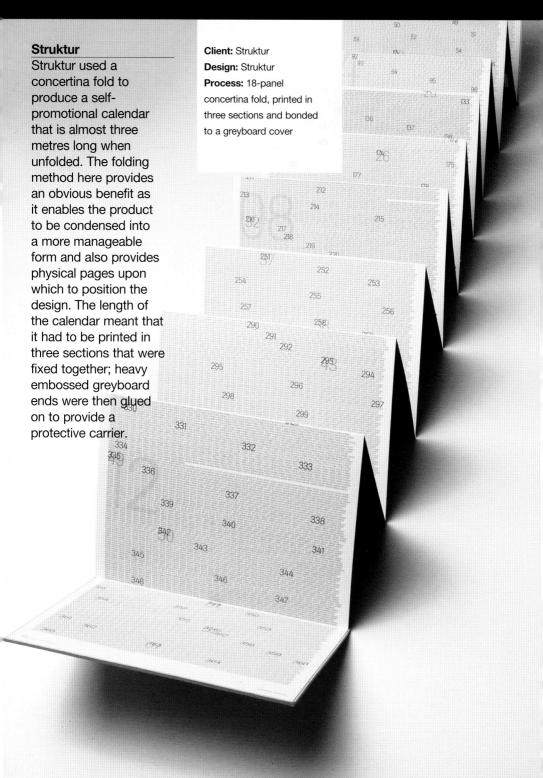

Client: FunLab
Design: KesselsKramer
Process: 12-panel concertina, bonded to outer die-cut wrap-cover

FunLab

For 'The Suitcase' project at the Eindhoven Design Academy in the Netherlands, KesselsKramer created a brochure with a concertina fold that emulates a suitcase – the contents spill out when it is opened. The end page is die cut so that it can be wrapped around the folded brochure to close it. The brochure documents a project in which students used the possessions from a suitcase they were given to construct a personality for a fictional character.

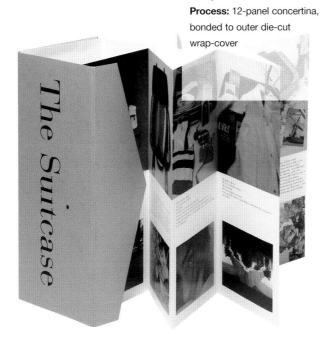

Different types of fold | Types of binding

Concertina fold

Each fold runs opposite to the previous one to obtain a pleated result. The outer page needs to be larger than the inner pages (as shown below) to hide the rough folding edges of the final piece. Alternatively, a concertina can be folded in on itself, in which case the pages can be made incrementally smaller. The weight and type of paper have a bearing on this measurement.

Outer page is fractionally larger to hide the pages below

x + 1–2mm   x   x   x

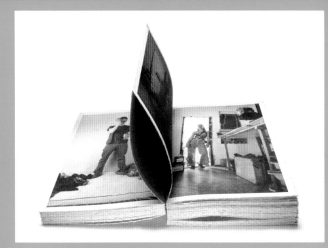

Different types of fold

Mined

In its design for *Mined* magazine, Tank used a variety of formatting techniques. The publication is made from eight sheets of paper, accordion-folded into 32-page sections and sewn into a book block. The book block is without a cover so that the stitching is exposed and becomes a feature of the design, rather than being hidden away as it usually is.

The outer fold on each page is perforated, enabling readers to tear pages open to reveal the complete pagination. The gradual tearing that this process requires leaves the book increasingly ragged on the outer edge. Each copy of the publication thereby bears the marks of individual readers and their use of it.

Accordion fold

Two or more parallel folds that go in opposite directions and open out like an accordion. Also called a concertina fold.

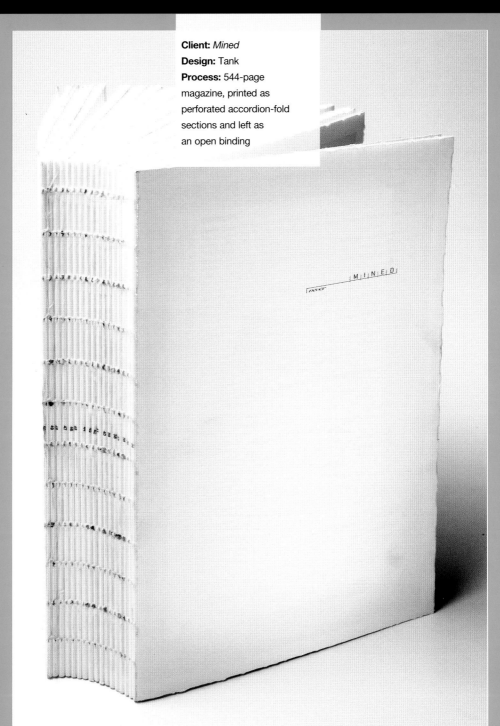

Client: *Mined*
Design: Tank
Process: 544-page
magazine, printed as
perforated accordion-fold
sections and left as
an open binding

The Image Bank

This spirit guide (a book outlining the aspirations and values of a brand) for stock photography library The Image Bank introduces a new identity, typographic style and outlines for image usage. As a means to organize information, the guide has a clear yet engaging narrative. The outer face of the folded sheets carries the main messages of the guide, while the inner reveals use increasingly more experimental interpretations of the typographic style.

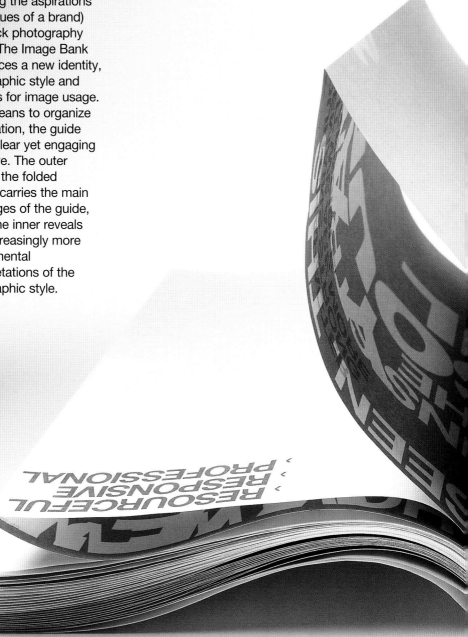

Client: The Image Bank
Design: North
Process: 74-page, French-fold
brochure, printed on thin stock
enabling showthrough

Different types of fold | Types of binding

Types of binding

Book and magazine binding can present a varied set of choices, ranging from the utilitarian staple through to more elaborate formats. In this section, we will explore how designers have used these techniques to great visual and tactile effect.

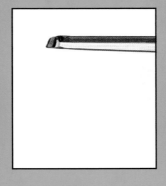

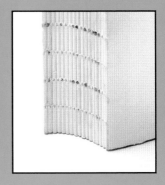

Informal
There are many types of informal binding, including elastic bands (shown above), clips and bolts.

Edition binding
Case or edition binding has signatures, or sections, of a book sewn together and bound with a cloth strip down the spine. This is then attached to endpapers, in turn connecting the text block to hard outer covers. This outer cover is then often 'wrapped' in a dust jacket for added protection.

Open binding
A form of binding where the collated, sewn signatures are left exposed, adding a dramatic graphic effect.

Perfect binding

A binding method commonly used for paperback books, where the signatures are held together with a flexible adhesive that also attaches a paper cover to the spine. The fore-edge is trimmed flat.

Saddle-stitch

A binding method used for booklets, programmes and small catalogues. Signatures are nested and wire stitches are applied through the spine along the centrefold. When opened, saddle-stitched books lay flat.

Wiro / comb-binding

A spine of metal (wiro) or plastic (comb) rings that binds and allows a document to open flat. Used for reports, office publications, manuals and so on. Usually with a hard-cover stock.

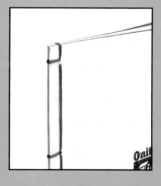

French fold

A sheet of paper that has two right-angle folds to form a four-page, uncut section. The section is sewn through the fold while the top edges remain folded and untrimmed. It's common for the inner reveals to be printed with a flood colour.

Canadian / half-Canadian binding

A spiral-bound volume with a wraparound cover that gives the benefits of spiral binding (lays flat, pages can be folded around) with the professional look of perfect binding. Half-Canadian has an exposed spine; a full Canadian has a covered spine.

Japanese or stab binding

A binding method whereby the pages are sewn together with one continual thread. Pages do not open flat. This is a very decorative binding method, which is not commonly used but is very luxurious.

Different types of fold | **Types of binding** | Print finishing

Booth-Clibborn Editions

Various different methods for book binding exist, including perfect, lay-flat and edition. This design by Form® for Booth-Clibborn Editions' publication *Rankin Works* uses edition binding, a method that gives the product a long life and allows the pages to lay flat when the book is opened. Hardback publications like this usually have a dust jacket. Originally, they offered protection against dirt and dust as the name suggests, but more recently they have become an integral graphic extension of the book and a key device for promotion.

Client: Booth-Clibborn Editions
Design: Form®
Process: Four-colour, edition-bound book

Different types of fold | **Types of binding** | Print finishing

Edition binding

Case or edition binding is a common hard-cover book-binding method whereby the signatures are sewn together, the spine is flattened, endsheets are applied and a cloth strip is added to the spine. The hard covers are then attached. The spine is usually rounded and grooves are made along the cover edge to act as hinges.

Headband/tailband

A headband or tailband is a piece of cloth tape that covers the top or bottom of the spine. It has both a decorative function and provides protection to the spine.

endpapers
headband
spine
dust jacket
tailband

Millennium Lofts

This brochure for Millennium Lofts' 9, Kean Street development designed by Cartlidge Levene is a two-section publication connected by a perforated z-bind.

The front section uses the strong colour photography of Covent Garden by Gueorgui Pinkhassov, who was commissioned by the client to spend a week in Covent Garden to photograph the area. The back section has a more limited colour palette and contains information specific to the 22 lofts that comprise the development.

Client: Millennium Lofts
Design: Cartlidge Levene
Process: 44- and 32-page brochures connected with perforated z-bind cover

Z-binds and perforated z-binds

Z-binds are a dual-binding technique, where two books are essentially bound onto a single cover. In the case of a perforated z-bind, these are pre-cut, indicating that the two parts are intended to be separated.

Client: Hub
Design: NB: Studio
Process: 148-page
catalogue printed onto a
stock which is coated on one
side and uncoated on the
reverse. Left with an open bind

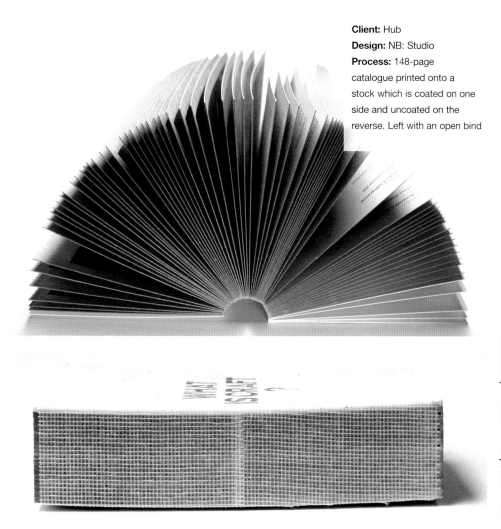

Different types of fold | **Types of binding** | Print finishing

Hub

This catalogue by NB: Studio for Hub, a centre for craft design and making in the UK, is essentially a series of heavyweight postcards bound into a book format. No cover is applied to the spine, creating a sculptural appearance to the publication.

Open binds

An open bind has a result like a book without its final cover-board applied. The glue and fabric used to secure pages is left exposed, creating a strong graphic statement.

Client: Stockport Arts and Health
Design: Eg.G
Process: Half-Canadian binding

Stockport Arts and Health

This collection of poetry by senior citizens was designed by Eg.G for Stockport Arts and Health, UK, and uses a half-Canadian binding.

Canadian and half-Canadian binding

In a full Canadian bind, the spirals that contain the document are completely hidden. In a half-Canadian bind (as above) they are left partially exposed. This is essentially a spiral-bound document, but with the advantage of having a book-like spine. As with spiral-bound documents, they have the advantage of laying completely flat when in use.

Client: Onitsuka

Design: Eg.G

Process: Japanese-bound, loose-leaf, French-fold booklet with flock cover

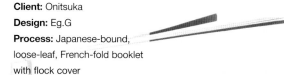

Onitsuka

This brochure for Onitsuka clothing company by Eg.G uses Japanese binding to provide a decorative element to the flock cover, both elements thereby reflecting the clothing trade that the client is involved in.

Different types of fold | **Types of binding** | Print finishing

Japanese binding

Japanese or stab binding is a binding method whereby pages are sewn together with one continual thread. This creates a decorative feature, while also providing a strong and durable binding method.

Client: Fourth Estate
Design: Frost Design
Process: 42 loose-leaf boards, letterpressed both sides and sealed in a card box

Fourth Estate

Frost Design created a brochure without binding and without a cover for this catalogue for book publisher Fourth Estate. The heavyweight, loose-leaf cards have been letterpressed and are presented in a storage box. The stock choice provides greater durability – an important consideration given that the pages are loose-leaf.

Informal or loose-leaf binding

Along with traditional approaches to binding, there are many more informal ones. These include innovative approaches, as shown opposite and on the following spread, and simpler, loose-leaf approaches, as above.

Sonneti

Using a die cut to make a series of small notches at the head and tail of the spine for this catalogue results in a distinctive bind. An elastic band stretched between the notches seals the piece, though without the degree of permanence that a binding usually confers. As no folio numbers were included on the pages, the brochure can easily be taken apart and tailored to suit individual tastes. The cover is made from a piece of board with six folds that are glued to form a spine. The size of these spine folds provides the appropriate capacity to hold the pages of the publication. Die-cut notches are found at the head and tail.

Client: Sonneti
Design: MadeThought
Process: Five-colour litho board, folded and glued with die-cut notches for elastic-band binding

Different types of fold | **Types of binding** | Print finishing

Capacity

When planning a publication, a designer needs to take into account the capacity of a cover to contain its pages. The dimensions of the spine will vary depending upon the number of pages in the publication. This is particularly true for perfect-bound publications and bindings, like the one in the example shown here.

Spring
Collec

Crafts Council

To illustrate how an innovative piece of flexible furniture works, designer John Rushworth perforated the back page of this exhibition catalogue so that readers can separate and rearrange photos of the pieces, then bind them with an elastic band to create a flip-book that animates the furniture. The colour scheme used for the catalogue was inspired by some of the key exhibition pieces.

Animation

Whether created online, for film or for cartoons, animation is typically produced from a series of still images each subtly different from those previous, which create the effect of movement when viewed at speed.

Client: Crafts Council
Design: Pentagram
(John Rushworth)
Process: Perforated brochure
that can be reconstructed into
a flip-book

13a

Print finishing

In addition to the different methods of folding and binding we have just explored, there also exists a range of print-finishing techniques which can be used to enhance and enliven a piece of work.

Anni Kuan

The fashion world is constantly in pursuit of the unique in order to create objects that both catch the eye and differentiate them in a crowded marketplace. Anni Kuan, a New York fashion designer, had a truly unique piece created for her by Sagmeister Inc. The loose-leaf broadsheet brochure hangs on a wire coat hanger and each page has been subjected to some very bespoke print finishing – by being burnt with an iron! It took five minutes to burn each of the brochure's 16 pages.

Client: Anni Kuan
Design: Sagmeister Inc.
Process: Four-colour litho
loose-leaf brochure,
hand-burnt with an iron and
packaged using a coat hanger

Types of binding | **Print finishing** | Industry view: Studio Output

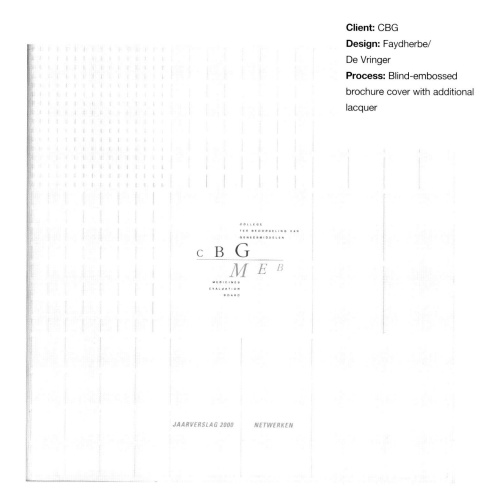

Client: CBG
Design: Faydherbe/
De Vringer
Process: Blind-embossed
brochure cover with additional
lacquer

CBG

The subtle tone-on-tone effect that can be produced by embossing is a key part of this design by Faydherbe/De Vringer for the Netherlands' CBG Medicines Evaluation Board annual report.

Embossing and debossing

An emboss is a design stamped into a substrate without ink or foil, resulting in a raised surface. When a stamp is used to give a recessed surface, the process is called debossing. The two processes are used to give decorative, textured effects to a publication and are typically used to provide emphasis to certain elements of the design. An emboss used on an uninked area is sometimes called 'blind embossing'.

Client: Beaux Arts
Design: Studio AS
Process: Four-colour litho with die-cut cover printed in silver

Beaux Arts

For a collection of David Spiller paintings that all featured circles, Studio AS used a die cut to hint at what lies within the catalogue rather than simply relying on an image.

Types of binding | **Print finishing** | Industry view: Studio Output

Client: Boym Partners/
Princeton Architectural Press
Design: Karlssonwilker Inc.
Process: Four-colour litho
brochure with die-cut handle

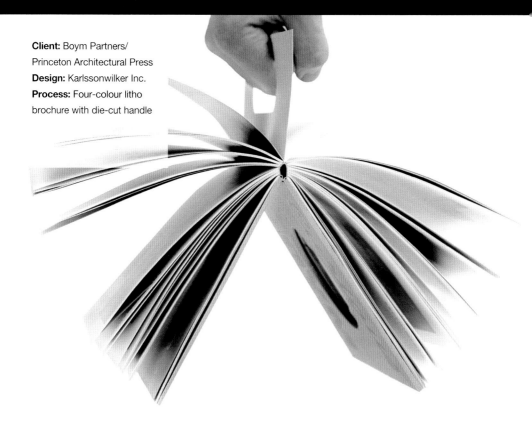

Boym Partners/Princeton Architectural Press

In its design scheme for a book about the industrial design studio Boym Partners for Princeton Architectural Press, Karlssonwilker Inc. killed two birds with one stone by putting a die-cut hole in the front cover. In addition to providing a glimpse inside the book, the removed cover stock was used as the book-launch party's invite/drinks coaster. The design also includes an innovative carry handle hidden between the centre pages.

Die cut

A process that uses a steel die to cut away a section of a page. Die cuts have many uses and are mainly used for decorative purposes to enhance the visual performance of a design. However, they may also serve a physical function, such as by making unusual shapes or creating apertures that allow users to see inside a publication. Die cuts produce a range of effects from the striking to the subtle. The front cover of this book has a die cut revealing the colour of the first page of the text block. More subtle applications include rounded die-cut corners, making printed matter physically 'softer' (see page 114).

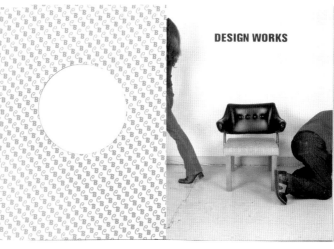

DESIGN WORKS

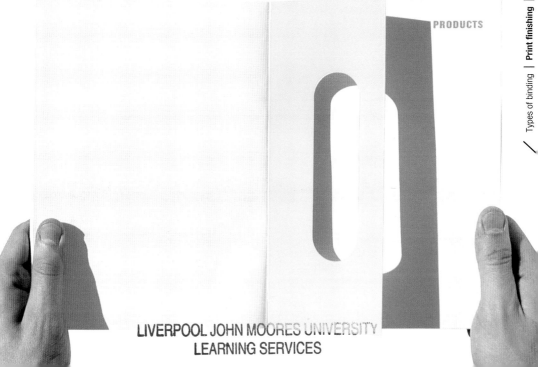

PRODUCTS

LIVERPOOL JOHN MOORES UNIVERSITY
LEARNING SERVICES

Client: Levi's® RED™
Design: The Kitchen
Process: 16-page four-colour litho die-cut brochure with metallic cover

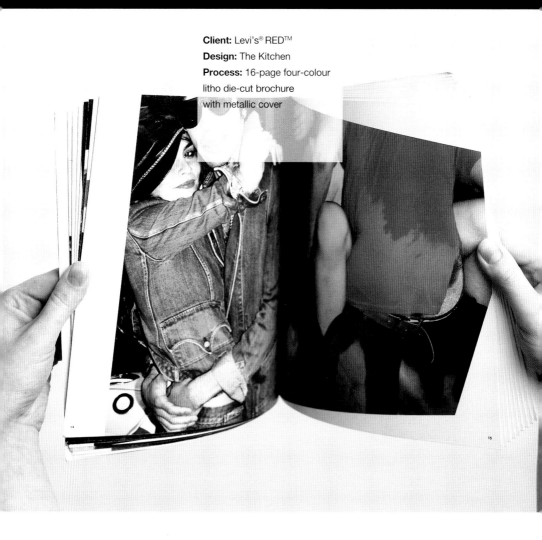

Levi's® RED™

The design tenet that 'form follows function' was a challenge for The Kitchen when creating a press brochure for Levi's® RED™ jeans, given that the trend for the season in question was 'twisted'. Its solution was to individually cut the 16 pages of the publication to create the illusion that the book is twisting as you flick through it. A metallic cover completes the piece.

Client: Struktur Design
Design: Struktur Design
Process: Two 32-page
saddle-stitched sections,
one eight-panel folded
cover, one elastic band

Types of binding | **Print finishing** | Industry view: Studio Output

Struktur Design

Not all forms of print finishing need to be expensive
or done by a specialist. There are many 'lo-fi' ways
of adding to a design, as Struktur's book *Hours*
demonstrates. Half of the book presents a calendar of
hours, while the other half comprises paintings made
by an artist created within a certain amount of time,
which get quicker as the minutes disappear. Each part
is produced as a separate book and both are then
bound together by an elastic band, alluding to the
elasticity of time.

Client: Lisa Pritchard Agency
Design: SEA Design
Process: Four-colour litho with die-cut corners

Lisa Pritchard Agency

In this range of stationery for the Lisa Pritchard Agency in London, SEA Design produced a simple design dominated by the large scale of the typography. The roundness of the typographic characters is mirrored by the die-cut corners.

Kiss cut

This is a method of die cutting whereby the face material of a self-adhesive substrate is die cut but not right through to the backing sheet. This enables the face material to be easily removed from the backing sheet.

Client: The Rolling Stones

Design: Sagmeister Inc.

Process: Filigree slipcase CD packaging

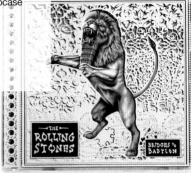

The Rolling Stones

This cover for The Rolling Stones' *Bridges to Babylon* CD, designed by Stefan Sagmeister and Hjalti Karlsson, features an illustration of an Assyrian lion by Kevin Murphy. The illustration is emphasized by a special filigree slipcase that outlines the lion with an intricate arabesque detail.

Types of binding | **Print finishing** | Industry view: Studio Output

Filigree

Filigree is traditionally ornamental work in which fine gold or silver wire is used to create intricate patterns.

Client: Photonica
Design: Frost Design
Process: Concertina-folded
with 'stamps' of perforated
type forming the logotype

Photonica

The versatility of the mailer format can be seen in this example by Frost Design for the Photonica photo library. Catering for the physical size and weight constraints that arise from the fact it is designed for mailing, it sacrifices nothing in terms of creativity or communication. A small selection of the images from the photo library are displayed in the piece courtesy of a concertina-fold pull-out. This folded section is bonded into a card wrap-folder that presents a more convenient size for sending through the post. The four-colour design is perforated, like a sheet of stamps, allowing the images to be separated and used like swatches – providing an indication of the usage and variety of the full library of images.

Types of perforation
A series of cuts or holes manufactured on a form to weaken it for tearing. Press perforation or machine perforation refer to how the perforation is made, while blade perforation and wheel perforation reference the cutting device used.

Types of binding | **Print finishing** | Industry view: Studio Output

Client: Bristol Regeneration Partnership
Design: Thirteen
Process: Silk-screened greyboard outer cover that doubles as an envelope

Bristol Regeneration Partnership

This annual report, designed by Thirteen, comprises an A5-format book stitched into its own mailable self-sealing greyboard envelope to reduce postage costs. Being perforated, the top and bottom flaps can be removed upon receipt, so that the object sheds its postal skin and functions purely as a book.

Client: NEROC'VGM

Design: KesselsKramer

Process: Four-colour
one side, single-colour on
reverse, perforated

NEROC'VGM

This is a book designed by KesselsKramer for the NEROC'VGM series of books
by artists exploring the theme of meeting, featuring 'A Meeting on Holiday,
Postcardland' by Joachim Schmid. Schmid sifted through thousands of images
and arranged the ones in this book into a kind of visual poetry. Each page has a
series of circular perforations through the middle and up the spine edge so that the
images become tear-out postcards.

Client: Haworth
Design: North
Process: Four-colour brochure, gatefold back cover, several throws, spot varnish, poster wrap

Haworth

This design for *tutti work architecture* by North is a poster-wrapped publication that contains a number of throws and a three-panel gatefold back cover. The brochure explores how changes to the physical work environment can alter and foster a more productive working culture in an organization. The bar design appears throughout the publication, sometimes as a graphic and other times as a more subtle spot varnish.

Spot varnish

Spot varnishing is the application of varnish to a specific area of a printed piece, usually providing full coverage of an image. In-line or 'wet' varnishing as a fifth or sixth colour during printing adds a wet layer of varnish onto a wet layer of ink. As they dry, they absorb into the stock together which diminishes the impact. Off-line varnishing applies the varnish as a separate pass once the inks have dried and results in extra glossiness, as less is absorbed by the stock. A UV spot varnish is a high-gloss varnish applied to selected areas to enhance impact or form part of the graphic design, and results in a raised texture.

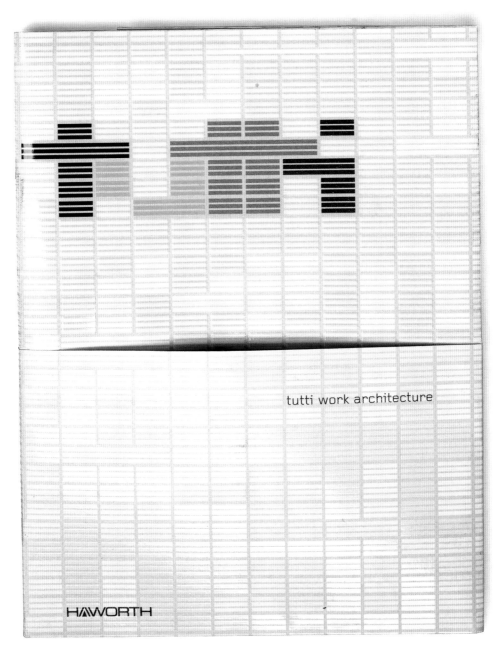

tutti work architecture

H/\WORTH

Industry view: Studio Output

This brochure for the UK Cultural Olympiad entitled *Igniting Ambition* uses a bespoke format to deliver an innovative and captivating piece of communication. The dramatic imagery by John Higgison shows Olympic hopefuls in iconic regional settings – and successfully combines sport and art.

This design uses a wrap-around cover. Can you explain why this solution was chosen as a form of binding?

The client had a limited budget with which to achieve a custom finish. Because mailing the booklet wasn't a requirement, we worked with our printer to find a format which made the most efficient use of the sheet, while changing the A-size proportions to something slightly more portrait and less standard. The wrap-around cover was also a way of using a standard process to create something slightly more bespoke. It's a common trick, but meant we could hide the standard saddle-stitched binding, resulting in a capacity spine which gives the booklet more presence.

Studio Output work across a range of media including print, moving image and film. Are there approaches to design that are transferable from one media to another?

To a certain extent, the approach is the same no matter what the media: we analyse the brief, conduct research and then generate ideas which get developed across various formats. But there are also specific approaches which might be driven by a certain technology or technique, so in that respect it's important to have specialists in each area who can share that knowledge. It helps everyone to have an understanding of what the other does!

Studio Output is a UK creative company working in every medium and operating as one team working across two studios in London and Nottingham. They work with innovative and interesting clients who appreciate their collaborative approach, including Sony Music, BBC, Sony PlayStation, Universal Pictures and Ministry of Sound. **www.studio-output.com**

A wrap-around cover forms a key part of this
design, creating both a containing device, and
also showcasing the imagery.

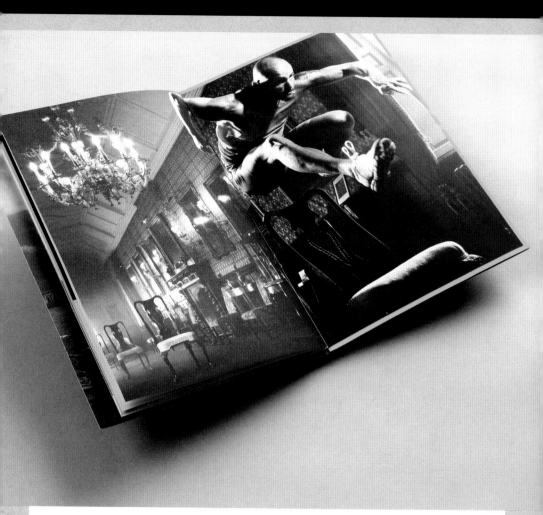

The images of athletes by John Higgison make a dramatic and dynamic impact. Was the format of the piece based around these images, or were the images shot specifically?

We'd already devised the format of the booklet and were considering options for what to wrap around the inside cover, such as infographics and maps. The client said that they had access to these images, which had been commissioned by East Midlands Tourism but which were only really seen in prominent large-format locations, such as airports. We thought that the subject matter and quality of these images sent out such a positive message about the region that they couldn't be ignored. The whole idea of the Cultural Olympiad is to unite sport and the arts. To us, these images achieve that beautifully.

Design activity:
Paper engineering

Premise
As we have seen throughout this chapter, paper engineering is a useful skill for a designer. Understanding how paper folds and how it can be bound and manipulated can enable you to make a point of difference in a design, as well as to control the order and reveal of information.

Exercise
1 Take an existing printed item and reappropriate the information using different folding arrangements.

2 Use either a business card, recipe or book and consider how different folds can be used to achieve a hierarchy in a design.

Aim
To produce a series of experimental, folded results.

Outcome
You will now have come to appreciate how folding and paper engineering are an integral part of the design process.

Suggested reading
- *Paper Engineering: 3-D Design Techniques for a 2-D Material* by Natalie Avella (Rotovision, 2006)
- *Pop-Up Design and Paper Mechanics* by Duncan Birmingham (GMC, 2010)
- *Paper: Tear, Fold, Rip, Crease, Cut* by Paul Sloman (Black Dog Publishing, 2009)
- *Papercraft: Design and Art with Paper* by Robert Klanten, S. Ehmann and B. Meyer (Die Gestalten Verlag, 2009)
- *Folding Techniques for Designers: From Sheet to Form* by Paul Jackson (Laurence King, 2011)

Industry view: Studio Output | Design activity: Paper engineering

Client: Alfaro Hofmann
Design: Lavernia & Cienfuegos
Process: Cut-out images on a standard identity suite

ALFARO HOFMANN
COLECCIÓN

COLECCIÓN ALFARO HOFMANN

Colección de electrodomésticos
Exposiciones temporales
Biblioteca

Fusters s/n. Pol. d'Obradors
46110 Godella · Valencia · Spain
Tel: +34 963 160 364
Fax: +34 963 160 361
coleccion@alfarohofmann.com
www.alfarohofmann.com

Colección de electrodomésticos
Exposiciones temporales
Biblioteca

Fusters s/n. Pol. d'Obradors
46110 Godella · Valencia · Spain
Tel: +34 963 160 364
Fax: +34 963 160 361
coleccion@alfarohofmann.com
www.alfarohofmann.com

Colección de electrodomésticos
Exposiciones temporales
Biblioteca

Fusters s/n. Pol. d'Obradors
46110 Godella · Valencia · Spain
Tel: +34 963 160 364
Fax: +34 963 160 361
coleccion@alfarohofmann.com
www.alfarohofmann.com

Colección de electrodomésticos
Exposiciones temporales
Biblioteca

Fusters s/n. Pol. d'Obradors
46110 Godella · Valencia · Spain
Tel: +34 963 160 364
Fax: +34 963 160 361
coleccion@alfarohofmann.com
www.alfarohofmann.com

ALFARO HOFMANN
COLECCIÓN

Chapter 4
Identity and branding

The terms identity and branding have become relatively interchangeable over time. Identity refers to what something looks like, through the colours and type styles that have been used. Branding is an expression of values in a product or service.

Through the use of corporate identity, you can establish a unique quality for your design. The typeface selected, how the type is set, and the stocks and printing techniques used will all have an impact on the overall identity of a piece. By instilling a set of values – branding – you can generate emotional relationships with end users. While identity gives you the tools to create a unique design, branding offers you a longer-term, emotional proposition as to what makes your product or service 'different'.

'A brand is a living entity – and it is enriched or undermined cumulatively over time, the product of a thousand small gestures.'

Michael Eisner

Construction | **Identity and branding** | Shape and form

Alfaro Hofmann

This identity suite for Alfaro Hofmann by Lavernia & Cienfuegos Diseño demonstrates how even the humble business card can become an object of desire. Reproduced cut-out images of Hofmann's collections of electrical designs combine with an avant-garde-style typeface to evoke the 'golden age' of small electrical appliances.

Stocks

The feel of printed items has an effect on how we respond to them, and on how we build a sense of identity and brand.

Standard paper uses

Paper type	Notes	Primary uses
Newsprint	Paper made primarily of mechanically ground wood pulp, shorter lifespan than other papers, cheap to produce, least expensive paper that can withstand normal printing processes.	Newspapers, comics.
Antique	Roughest finish offered on offset paper.	To add texture to publications such as annual reports.
Uncoated wood-free	Largest printing and writing paper category by capacity that includes almost all office and offset grades used for general commercial printing.	Office paper (printer and photocopy paper, stationery).
Mechanical	Produced using wood pulp, contains acidic lignins. Suitable for short-term uses as it will 'yellow' and colours will fade.	Newspapers, directories.
Art board	Uncoated board.	Cover stock.
Art	A high-quality paper with a clay filler to give a good printing surface, especially for half-tones where definition and detail are important. Has high brightness and gloss.	Colour printing, magazines.
Cast-coated	Coated paper with a high-gloss finish obtained while the wet-coated paper is pressed or cast against a polished, hot, metal drum.	High-quality colour printing.
Chromo	A waterproof coating on a single side, intended for good embossing and varnishing performance.	Labels, wrappings, and covers.
Cartridge	A thick white paper used particularly for pencil and ink drawings.	To add texture to publications such as annual reports.
Greyboard	Lined or unlined board made from waste paper.	Packaging material.
Flock	Paper coated with flock; very fine woollen refuse or vegetable fibre dust that gives a velvety or cloth-like appearance.	Decorative covers.

Client: Black Dog Publishing
Design: Society
Process: Single-colour litho
with silk-screened greyboard
cover and endpapers with
buckram binding

Stocks | Colour

Black Dog Publishing

For this book, *City Racing, The Life and Times of an Artist-Run Gallery*, Society chose a greyboard cover to add grittiness to the publication and so reflect its content. The cover and the endpapers were silk-screened and a green buckram binding applied. The choice of stocks make a unique and powerful statement, as do the choice of typeface and colour.

Buckram

A coarse linen or cotton fabric stiffened with glue or gum used for covering a hard-cover binding.

Client: Clarke & Reilly
Design: Morse Studio
Process: Red and black
foiled greyboard invite

CLARKE & REILLY PRESENT
OF WORK BY 6 ARTISTS/CRA
BY THE DESIGNS OF FRANK LL
BY BRIDGET DWYER AND DAVID
FEATURING WORK BY MARY DW
JAMES PLUMB LIGHTING/CLARA VUL
MARTIN TUCKER FURNITURE/CLARA VUL
KIRSTEN HECKTERMANN/LUCY GR
EXHIBITION RUNS 22 OCTOBER—19 N
PRIVATE VIEW WEDNESDAY 21 OCTOBE

8 PORCHESTER PLACE LONDON W2 2HS
+44 (0)20 7262 3300 INFO@CLARKEANDREILLY.COM
WWW.CLARKEANDREILLY.COM

C&R

Clarke & Reilly

To mark the 50th anniversary of the death of Frank Lloyd Wright, Clarke & Reilly curated and hosted an exhibition of works inspired by the architect at their London showroom. The invites use a matte, red foil square (a reference to the mark that adorned Wright's drawings), stamped on a thick greyboard. Finer, typographic details are stamped in black foil, creating a strong typographic identity.

Stocks | Colour

Foil

Also known as a hot-foil stamp, this process uses heat to transfer metallic foil to a substrate. Foils range from flat colours to holographic patterns and add a tactile element to a design.

Client: Underware
Design: Faydherbe/
De Vringer
Process: Flock cover with
foil-blocked type and image

Underware

'Dolly' is an alternative typeface catalogue for a new typeface called 'Dolly', designed by Underware. Dolly is also the name of the canine character who features in the product's logo, which is foil-blocked onto the cover of the catalogue designed by Faydherbe/De Vringer and who is the protagonist of the catalogue's storyline.

Flock, a substrate that can take a foil-blocked logo and is sufficiently robust to be die cut to house the CD holder, was chosen for the cover, against which the textless, foil-stamped front cover is both intriguing and dramatic.

Stocks | Colour

Flock

This is paper coated with flock – very fine woollen refuse or vegetable fibre dust – that is fixed with glue or size to give the substrate a velvety or cloth-like appearance.

Foil stamp

A foil stamp is a foil or coloured tape that is pressed onto a substrate using heat and pressure.

Client: Anne Klein
Design: Karlssonwilker Inc.
Process: Single-colour print
utilizing showthrough

Showthrough
Showthrough or strikethrough is where printing inks can be seen on the reverse side of the page.
Particularly common with thin paper stocks and/or those with low loadings of fillers and coating, it is generally
considered undesirable but, as this example shows, it can be used creatively to interesting effect.

Anne Klein

Karlssonwilker Inc. designed a stationery system for Anne Klein, including this
letterhead. At first sight, it appears to be a standard letterhead on American letter
format paper. However, the logo on the letterhead is completed by the strikethrough
of a subtle band of colour printed on the reverse.

Client: OXO
Design: Tank
Process: Wiro-bound, four-colour book with laminated pages and a metal cover stock

Sausage Cassoulet

OXO

For this cookbook for OXO, Tank focused on how such publications are typically used and endeavoured to create a more user-friendly format. A magnetized metal substrate was chosen for the cover, enabling the cookbook to be stuck to the fridge. The pages are laminated in order that static electricity holds them to each other so that they don't flip over whilst suspended, which also enables them to be wiped clean. Another inspired touch is that each recipe has the ingredients printed onto a Post-it®-style note that can be removed and taken by the reader to the supermarket. This example shows how thinking about design in relation to product use, paper choices and mechanics can create both functional and inspirational results.

Stocks | Colour

Colour

Colour can have a dramatic effect on a design, and is often exploited as a design tool. Many companies and products are identifiable through colour alone. Taking ownership of a specific colour, be it subtle or bold, can be a powerful way of generating customer alliance and retention. Often, designers will use a colour wheel to work out where competitors fit into an often crowded marketplace and which segments of it, if any, remain free. An alternative approach is to simply imitate the colour choices of rival brands. Many own-brand colas, for instance, mimic the red of the bestselling brand, Coca-Cola – thereby aligning themselves with the larger brand in an attempt to profit by this association.

Warm

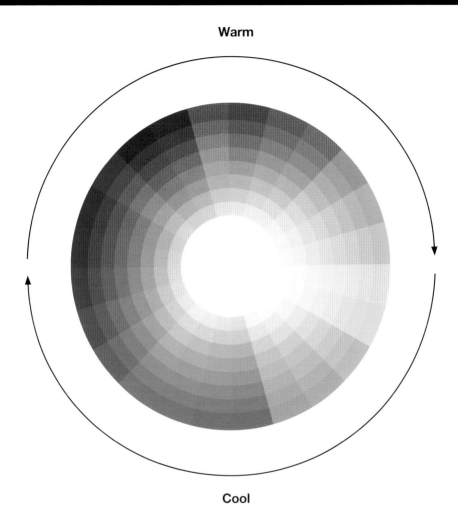

Cool

Shown above is a circular representation of a colour wheel. These are used to both select colours, and to identify areas or zones that aren't being used in a marketplace. Brands often take one of two approaches. Firstly, you can use a colour wheel to plot, or place all your competitors on, identifying any clusters, and importantly any gaps that can be exploited. Alternatively, brands will sometimes try to blend in with competitors, meaning that you identify what colours are appropriate for certain markets and stick within that colour range. This is most commonly seen in packaging design, where certain products share certain key colours, for example the cool greens and blues of dental care products.

In simple terms, the wheel can essentially be divided in two, with half the colours being described as 'warm' and the other half being referred to as 'cool'.

Client: Design Museum
Design: Studio Myerscough
Process: Die-cut invitation
printed with graduating colour

RSVP on 020 7940 8783
or membership@designmuseum.org
www.designmuseum.org

Design Museum

Colour, typographic
style, paper stocks and
shape can all significantly
contribute to the successful
creation of an identity and brand.
For the Somewhere Totally Else
exhibition at the Design Museum in
London, Studio Myerscough created an invite
with die-cut letterforms. The graduated printed
colour forms a crucial part of the identity of the show.

Client: The Belgian Chocolate
Mousse Company
Design: The Collective
Process: Subtle use of foils
and careful colour selection

The Belgian Chocolate Mousse Company

Margaret Nolan of The Collective used a carefully selected colour range and printing techniques to craft this strong visual identity. The main typographical titling is reproduced in a subtle matte white foil, with secondary typographical elements printing in grey. These are all reversed out of a special blue. This attention to detailing, and the weighting and typeface selection creates an instantly recognizable brand.

Client: West Architecture
Design: Morse Studio
Process: Use of negative space and colour to create a strong visual identity

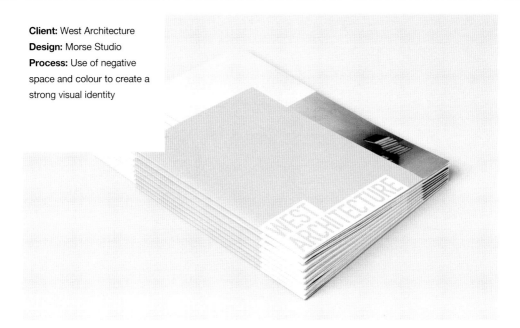

The identity's use of logo
positioning is extended onto
stationery. Precision and care
are taken to carefully execute
the design.

West Architecture

This identity makes
explicit use of negative
space and colour
to create a visually
arresting identity. The
logo positioning in
the bottom left-hand
corner of the printed
and on-screen page
activates the space
and creates a sense of
dynamism. The brochure
features an innovative
reverse-folded cover.

The Citigroup Private Bank

This print collateral for The Citigroup Private Bank Australian Photographic Prize uses a combination of stocks and printing techniques to create a subtle, understated effect. The outer containers, boxes and envelopes use a silver stock, that has typography applied as a debossed silver foil. This silver-on-silver process creates a strong identity and sense of modern simplicity. The accompanying photographic images are printed CMYK onto a smooth, high white stock.

Client: The Citigroup
Private Bank
Design: The Collective
Process: Silver foiled and
debossed typography on
silver stock

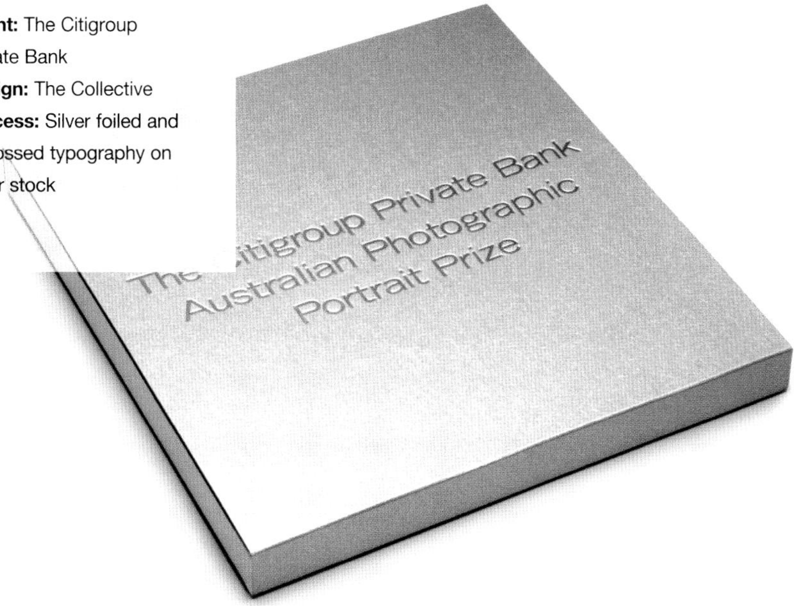

The Citigroup Private Bank
Australian Photographic
Portrait Prize

Client: Profusion
Design: The Kitchen
Process: Laser-cut stationery range with a subtle use of colour

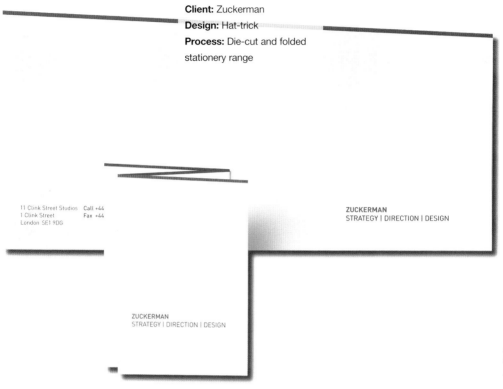

Client: Zuckerman

Design: Hat-trick

Process: Die-cut and folded stationery range

11 Clink Street Studios Call +44
1 Clink Street Fax +44
London SE1 9DG

ZUCKERMAN
STRATEGY | DIRECTION | DESIGN

ZUCKERMAN
STRATEGY | DIRECTION | DESIGN

Stocks | **Colour** | Industry view: Planning Unit

Profusion (page 144)

Creative destruction in design can produce both striking and effective results, as this business card by The Kitchen for client Profusion illustrates. A laser was used to burn a pattern of holes into the substrate. On a white stock such as this, the laser creates small burn rings around each hole. These burn rings can be hidden by overprinting with a solid colour but in this case, creative director Rob Petrie intentionally left them visible. The burn marks appear on the back of the card, as seen on the left of the photograph opposite. The cool, textured blue hues create a soft backdrop for the strong graphic intervention.

Zuckerman

This stationery package designed by Hat-trick design studio was tailored to the client Zuckerman by using the initial 'Z'. The format of each item was die cut on a bias to give a sloping top edge so that when folded – with a z-fold, naturally – the red stripe running along the top becomes a 'Z', as can be seen in the folded business card. Combined with the folding technique, the red stripe becomes the colour element that the company can take ownership of in the creation of their identity.

Industry view: Planning Unit

Planning Unit exploit creative possibilities in this events catalogue for the London International Documentary Festival (LIDF), produced in association with UpCreative. The resulting design makes use of flood colour pages to break up the content.

The guide has a strong sense of identity that makes use of the format of the book, wrapping around the spine, creating a sense of 'object' or value. Can you explain how you approach a design like this – does the identity drive the format, or is the format set out first?
The identity came first and became an integral part of the design. The brochure was one part of a number of applications, including posters, postcards, adverts and on-screen graphics, so by using the visual language we could create a harmonious brand-led body of work. To achieve this, the ingredients from the visual language were utilized – colours, typography and the graphic device on the cover and section dividers.

Do you ever feel restricted by a particular format structure, or do you see this as a crucial part of the design challenge – to create something dynamic in a relatively ordinary format or space?

Format can be a big part of the design process: when it's not predetermined it can offer up lots of possibilities; but when a format is decided it can in one respect be a challenge and on the other hand it can help guide the direction you go in. The really tricky situation is when the format is simply too small for the required purpose and content that is needed – that can become a frustrating challenge.

The outer cover and spreads create a sense of pace and order through the use of colour and image placement.

**The spreads in the event catalogue convey a sense of pace and activity, through their varied layout and use of 'breaker' sections, as shown below.
Is this something you actively try to instil as part of the design process?**

The grid is actually quite simple, the formatting of the different types of information is very strict, but we tried to make the positions within the layout as varied and dynamic as possible. This way you get something that has a sense of pace and activity, but also has a great deal of consistency and clarity. The breaker section served the purpose of making it engaging, and not repetitive. The brochure is actually split into three main sections: the front section, which is printed in fluoro orange, black and silver; the middle section, which is printed in full colour to carry the striking images; and the end section, which is printed in fluoro blue, black and silver.

With over twenty years' combined experience at London's top design agencies, Nick Hard and Jeff Knowles teamed up to launch their own creative design studio, Planning Unit. Their clients include Knoll, The Design Museum, BBC, PQ Eyewear, Twin Magazine and Xindao. **www.planningunit.co.uk**

Design activity:
Stocks and colour

Premise
Designers use stocks and colour to create a point of difference. In crowded markets, this is especially important and often the start of the design process is to conduct an audit of competitors and like-brands.

Exercise
Pick a market sector from within a supermarket. This could be skincare, dried goods, confectionery, etc. Conduct an audit of the most successful brands within this sector. Firstly, look at what stocks and printing devices they use. Is there a predominance of foils and other devices designed to catch the eye? Are there sectors that favour more subtle approaches? The stocks used can sometimes tell a story, or form a narrative about the story that a brand is conveying. For example, glossy, shiny packaging for organic or Fairtrade products might cause a conflict of messages. Secondly, what colours do they use? How are these different or distinct from other sectors? Consider the following:

• Are some colours inherently more 'appropriate' to particular sectors than others?

• Are some colours taboo or rarely used in a given market?

• How does the use of colour influence how we view and relate to products?

Aim
To encourage thinking about a design in a holistic, more rounded way. The feel of a design can have just as big an impact as the look.

Outcome
A series of research boards exploring a particular market sector.

Suggested reading
• *Paper Engineering: 3D Design Techniques for a 2D Material* by Natalie Avella (Rotovision, 2006)
• *Encyclopedia of Paper-Folding Designs* by Natsumi Akabane (PIE Books, 2005)
• *Papercraft: Design and Art with Paper* by Robert Klanten, S. Ehmann and B. Meyer (Die Gestalten Verlag, 2009)

Colour | Industry view: Planning Unit | Design activity: Stocks and colour

Client: Liberty
Design: SEA Design
Process: Etched acrylic invite

Chapter 5
Shape and form

Printed items can, at a certain point, become more concerned with packaging – by thinking of a design as an object or item, rather than simply printed paper. This chapter showcases examples of design that have transcended conventions and challenged manufacture, resulting in some visually stunning pieces of work.

Although this often involves the use of sophisticated print production techniques – for example lenticular and fore-edge printing – you'll also see that creative results can be achieved by simply thinking harder.

'Good design is making something intelligible and memorable.
Great design is making something memorable and meaningful.'

Dieter Rams

Identity and branding | **Shape and form** | New media

Liberty
SEA Design made an imaginative substrate choice for these invites for British fashion designer Matthew Williamson's 'Lifestyle' show at Liberty in London. Using acrylic of different colours, the simple, informative design is etched into the substrate. The format size also makes the invite suitable to use as a coaster.

Shape and form

The shape and form of printed items can become integral to their identity, as the example on page 153 shows. Ideas and brands can be generated through the innovative use of shape and the folding and forming of printed material. Although some formats are standard for obvious reasons, nothing stops a design from breaking out of these conventions.

Bailhache Labesse Group

This annual review for the Bailhache Labesse Group was created by Felton Communication Ltd. It consists of three different-sized, saddle-stitched publications, which are bound together and cover 'the past', 'the present' and 'the future' of the organization and share common elements. All have high-gloss covers with a spot-varnish border and use the subtle cropping of recurrent images to demonstrate the progression of time. The typography reflects the chronology of the brochures, with the past using a 'thin', the present using a 'regular' and the future using a 'bold' version of a single typeface.

Client: Bailhache
Labesse Group
Design: Felton
Communication
Process: Three saddle-
stitched brochures
bonded together

the present

Bailhache
Labesse
annual review
2002/2003

BaILHacHe
LaBeSSe
GROUP

Shape and form / series

The Imperial War Museum North

These invites and promotional CD cases for the Imperial War Museum use a series of die-cuts and folds to reflect the architecture of the iconic building. The shape of the invites creates a juxtaposition of angles with the photography. The Daniel Liebeskind building in Salford Quays is a celebration of shape and form, and this print material reflects this sense of pride.

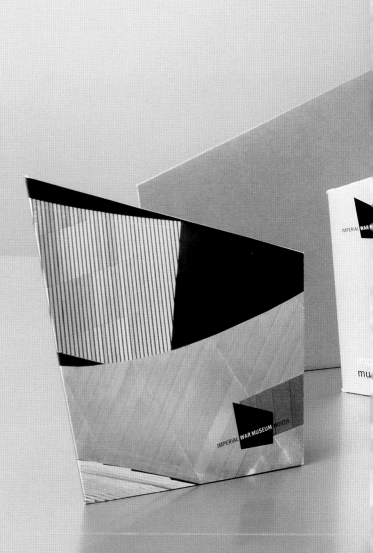

Client: The Imperial
War Museum North
Design: True North
Process: Die-cut
folded invites

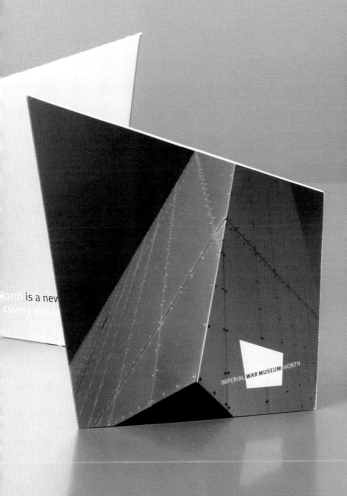

Client: Lord's Cricket Ground
Design: Cartlidge Levene
Process: Four-colour,
cut-board cover containing
four-colour inserts

Lord's Cricket Ground

This is a brochure for a building at the Lord's Cricket Ground in London by Future Systems. Cartlidge Levene designed a thick, covered board that forms a folder with a diagonal cut for an opening that wraps around the two sections that comprise the main body. Inside are two loose-leaf sections; one provides a photographic record of the construction project, while the other provides background information about it.

reader:

go forwards,
don't go backwards,
and remember,
many a true string
said in vest.

Multiple covers

Interest and collectability can be added to a publication by having multiple covers. This is common in magazine design, where special editions are released with a series of different covers. The example here reflects the eclectic nature of the book, and makes the book all the more personal and desirable.

Client: Violette Editions
Design: Aboud Creative
Process: Four-colour book with tip-ins cut to different sizes in polystyrene case with magnifying glass, loose-leaf posters and inserts

Shape and form | Series

Violette Editions

This book for British clothing designer Paul Smith, *You Can Find Inspiration in Everything* *And if You Can't, Look Again*, designed by Aboud Creative, is quite an interesting package. It comes in a polystyrene case with a magnifying glass and a pattern for a suit jacket that has multiple arms. The book itself has several tip-ins and multiple covers. The picture on page 158 shows the introduction page that has been cut to a different height than the regular pages and is written in multiple languages. The theme of the publication is discovery and excitement, which is portrayed through the various format choices that have been made.

LIVERPOOL JOHN MOORES UNIVERSITY
LEARNING SERVICES

Series

A sense of series or continuity can add collectability and value to a design. This sense of continuity can be introduced through photographic style, colour, paper stocks or an overall approach to a design.

Canongate Books Ltd.

Here is an example of a slipcase used for packaging several books together as one product. This project for Canongate Books Ltd. was to produce 12 extracts from the *King James Bible* in pocket form. Pentagram partner Angus Hyland approached the project as though he were designing covers for modern fiction, but used tonally dark stock photography to reflect the seriousness of the content and to avoid relying on a particular photographic style. The results include an image of a nuclear explosion for *Revelation*, and a Kafkaesque silhouette for the book of *Job*. Packaged separately as the 'Old Testament' and the 'New Testament', each group of six volumes is contained in a slipcase.

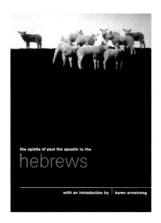

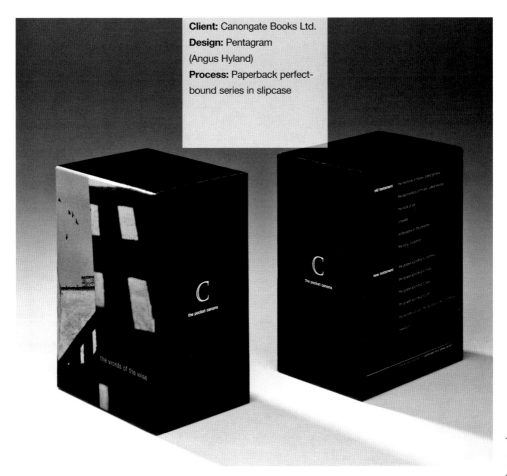

Client: Canongate Books Ltd.
Design: Pentagram
(Angus Hyland)
Process: Paperback perfect-
bound series in slipcase

Shape and form | **Series** | Book as sculpture

Client: Ministry of Sound
Design: Studio Output
Process: Model items, hand-painted and photographed in various studio locations

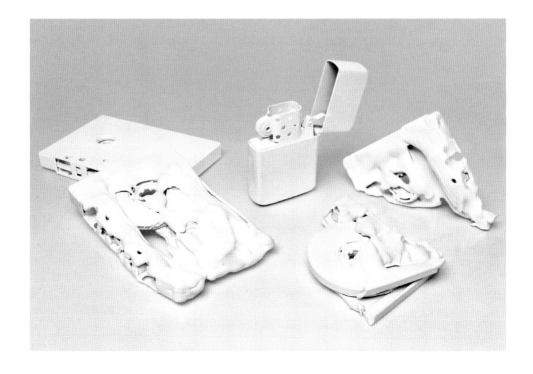

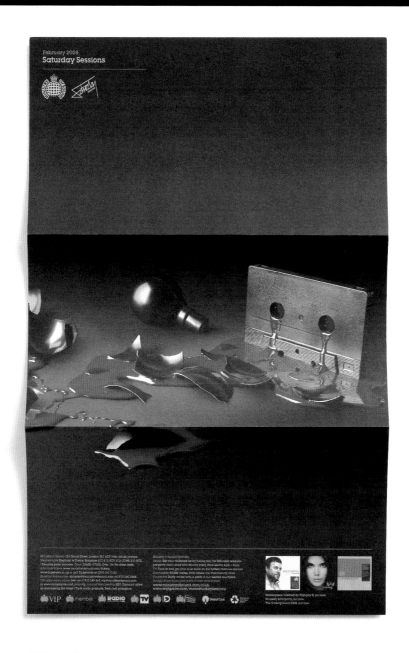

Ministry of Sound

These quarterly communications for the Ministry of Sound, London, use a thematic representation of music, in this case the casette tape. The 'death' of this medium is portrayed in a series of posters and flyers, creating an overall identity and innovative use of imagery.

Book as sculpture

The book has long since been revered as an object of art and beauty – and not merely as a collection of bound pages.

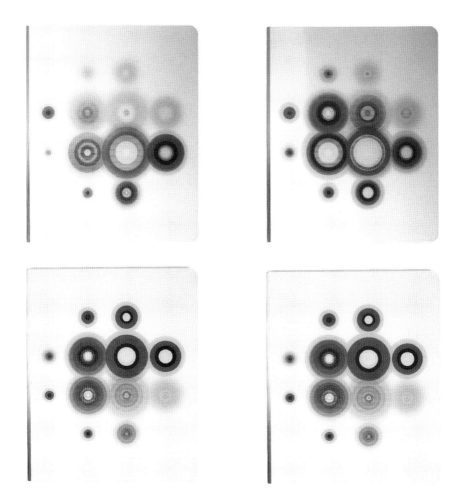

Client: Telewest
Design: North
Process: 124-page book,
die-cut corners, lenticular
cover front and back

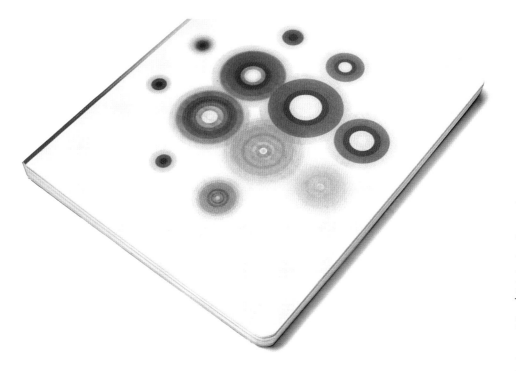

Telewest

Design studio North put a lenticular image on the front and rear covers of the Design Guidelines Brand Manual for Telewest. The cover image is the organization's logo, which moves and changes as the reader changes his or her viewing angle. This ties in with an animated version of the logo that appears in television commercials for the organization. The idea is very simple but also well-executed, transforming a corporate brochure into an object of desire.

Lenticular

A lenticular is a printed image that shows depth or motion as the viewing angle changes.

Client: Hans Brinker
Budget Hotel
Design: KesselsKramer
Process: Perfect-bound four-
colour brochure with centred
cross-cut pages

Hans Brinker Budget Hotel

This brochure by KesselsKramer for a hotel in Amsterdam has pages cut through the middle to create separate components that can be independently flipped under a flock cover. The theme of the imagery is that the guests are fine when they arrive but look the worse for wear when they leave, having had such a good time in Amsterdam. The separation allows an interactive juxtaposition of before-and-after images.

Client: Foruli Publishing
Design: Andy Vella
Process: Book printed on waterproof paper and sealed in stainless steel laser-etched time capsule

Foruli Publishing

This reinterpretation of a book for Foruli Publishing by Andy Vella is unusual as it is designed to last. The book is about the rise and fall of Factory Records, a seminal UK record label. The transcript of the book is printed on waterproof plastic paper, with a silk-screened cover. The entire contents are then presented in a stainless steel, airtight and watertight laser-etched time capsule.

Client: Mikael Eliasson
Design: Morse Studio
Process: Perfect-bound catalogue with taped spine

Mikael Eliasson

This catalogue was produced to accompany Eliasson's solo exhibition, Resemblance. The family portraits are printed on a rigid, uncoated card stock and arranged objectively across spreads with a delicate passepartout border. The juxtaposition of images simultaneously creates a sense of calm and a peculiar feeling of tension. The catalogue uses lay-flat binding, which is similar to perfect binding but instead uses a cold glue, and which combined with buckram book tape covering the spine enables the book's pages to lie flat when open.

Passepartout
A simple border or frame surrounding an image.

Industry view: Propaganda

Propaganda's approach to a new perfume packaging demonstrates how crucial shape and form are in crowded markets, where making a point of difference is vital.

Can you firstly explain how you might come to approach a design brief like this? For instance, does the name, the colour or the shape come first?

As part of our ongoing work with the cult beauty brand Illamasqua, we have been heavily involved in the creation, development and launch of their first fragrance. As a brand that celebrates the idiosyncrasy of people being unique and out of the ordinary, Illamasqua adopted the name 'Freak' for the first fragrance. Given this as a basis, we explored a range of different avenues for what a 'Freak' bottle should look like.

The design has some unique and unusual elements, not least the missing corner that creates a real point of difference. Can you elaborate on how you add meaning and narrative through shape, symbol and colour?

The bottle shape is based on a traditional classic perfume bottle, with the bottom right corner removed to make the bottle stand on its edge, echoing the Freak ethos of 'refusing to fit in'.

A silver snail is attached to the bottle, a snail being a creature that is perfectly formed yet not admired as being conventionally beautiful by the masses; this represents Illamasqua's love of beauty in all things, especially the unconventional.

Illamasqua considers itself a night-time brand, therefore it makes sense that this unisex fragrance is made from flowers that bloom only at night, including the Queen of the Night (or night-blooming cereus), a rare flowering cacti found in the American tropics, whose blooms are spent by sunrise.

Propaganda are business and brand strategists, marketing professionals, creatives and designers who use insights, knowledge and experience to transform business and brand equity working on everything from start-ups to some of the UK's biggest brands. Propaganda's clients include Illamasqua, Seabrooks, Boost drinks, Neal & Wolf and The Car People. **www.propaganda.co.uk**

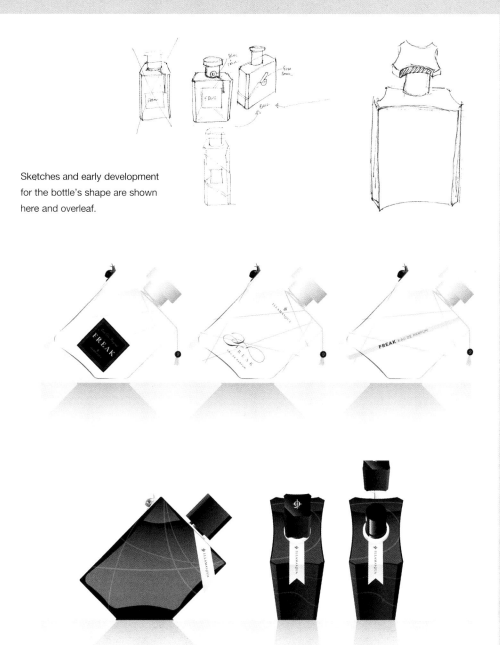

Sketches and early development for the bottle's shape are shown here and overleaf.

Left: Revised bottle shape, incorporating the 'angle' device.

Below: The final bottle design complete with snail adornment.

Design activity:
Adding value

Premise
In this chapter, we have seen many ways by which designers have added value and interest to a project or product, be they print materials, packaged items, or even the humble business card. Doing so can transform the ordinary into the magical and the dull into the interesting.

Exercise
1 Take a piece of found literature or packaging. This could be a timetable, a theatre guide, a book or a series of pamphlets.

2 Think about the subject matter and devise a series of methods for adding value to the original item.

3 Don't be restricted when considering what can be added. Think about paper stocks containing devices, materials and items that can accompany the original found object.

Aim
You will start thinking about printed material and packaged items not simply for what they are, but instead in terms of what they could be.

Outcome
To produce a series of experimental publications or packages which explore how you can add value and interest to a given design.

Suggested reading
- *New Packaging Design* by Janice Kirkpatrick (Laurence King, 2009)
- *Packaging the Brand: The Relationship Between Packaging Design and Brand Identity* by Gavin Ambrose and Paul Harris (AVA Publishing, 2011)
- *Experimental Formats / Experimental Packaging* by Daniel Mason and Roger Fawcett-Tang (Rotovision, 2004)

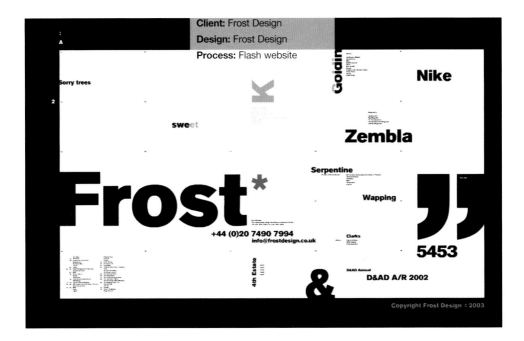

Client: Frost Design
Design: Frost Design
Process: Flash website

Chapter 6
New media

Technology convergence is beginning to result in information being viewed by users on multiple platforms and spaces. What once was static (posters on the underground or metro, for example) is now very much active and dynamic.

Websites are becoming populated with film, bringing together two mediums that were once very separate. We are also witnessing an advance in hand-held technology that will change the way we view content in a fundamental way. Designers working today need to face these contemporary challenges and strive to facilitate meaningful communication across a broader range of devices and platforms.

'True interactivity is not about clicking on icons or downloading files, it's about encouraging communication.'
Edwin Schlossberg

Shape and form | New media

Frost Design
When using a website, a user is typically looking for a certain piece of information. Navigation is the means whereby users can be directed towards different types of information. Frost Design has chosen to mimic print media in its website design. The visual effect is more what we would expect to see on a printed page than on a website. Initially, the design looks like a poster before the Flash animation begins.
www.frostdesign.co.uk

Film and moving image

A film is a series of moving or still images. These images form an initial story or an idea. Films are produced by recording photographic images with cameras, or by creating images using animation techniques, such as visual effects. The process of making films has developed not only into an art form, but also into an entire industry. Films today are not only considered to be cultural artefacts or powerful art forms, but are also seen as sources of popular entertainment and a strong method for both communicating and educating.

Virgin Records

why not associates decided against industry-standard film equipment to shoot an ident for Virgin Special Projects, preferring to use 16mm instead. This film format has its own unique aesthetic that imparts into the subject matter a vibrant grittiness akin to that of a road movie. This was enhanced with lots of post-production, including overlaid type and illustration.

Client: Virgin Records
Design: why not associates
Process: Post-produced
16mm film footage

Film and moving image | Websites and hand-helds

International Society for Human Rights

The project *The Typewriter* is a commercial production made by students of the Film Academy Baden-Wuerttemberg for the International Society for Human Rights. It is an impressive film about freedom of expression which raises awareness of the danger that journalists face when reporting on politically sensitive international issues. www.typewriter-spot.de

Client: International Society for Human Rights
Design: Andreas Roth, Florian Panier, Norman Scholl, Christian Hergenröther
Process: Short film that became a viral success

/ **Film and moving image** | Websites and hand-helds

Viral
If something goes viral, it means that it becomes extremely popular in a short amount of time, namely on the Internet. It is common for videos or emails to go viral via Internet sharing, typically through popular social media sites such as YouTube.

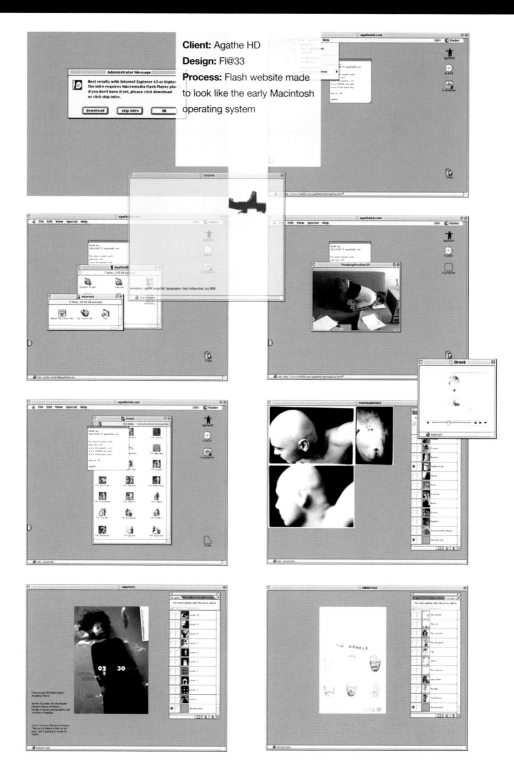

Client: Agathe HD
Design: Fl@33
Process: Flash website made to look like the early Macintosh operating system

Websites and hand-helds

The explosion of content on websites is unprecedented. Consumers now access music, watch film footage and browse web pages with a new-found freedom. These forms of content are gradually merging so that, as we saw on the previous spread for instance, online film can become a form of viral media, being shared and distributed at a speed never before possible.

Agathe HD

The appropriation and adaptation of other objects is nothing new. For her website, Agathe Jacquillat took the appearance of the Macintosh operating system as her inspiration and used it as the basis for her design. When viewed on a Macintosh, this creates a 'screen' within the screen. The appropriation of the visual appearance of software is also used elsewhere in the site; the portfolio section, for instance, is designed to look like the layers palette in Photoshop.

www.agathehd.com

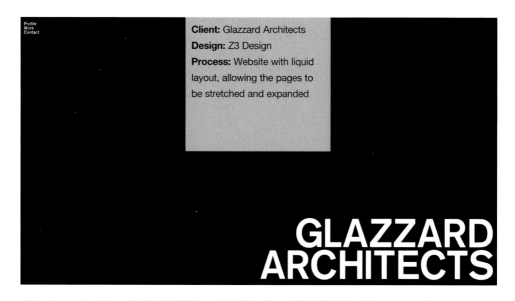

Profile
Work
Contact

Client: Glazzard Architects

Design: Z3 Design

Process: Website with liquid layout, allowing the pages to be stretched and expanded

GLAZZARD
ARCHITECTS

Glazzard Architects

This website by Z3 Design for Glazzard Architects uses a liquid layout to make a strong graphic statement. The position of the logo at the bottom right reinforces the identity, while the floating base image creates a dynamic and energetic visual statement.
www.glazzards.com

Next
Work
Home

MADE Youth Shelter, Worcester
A collaborative design project between young people,
architects and artists, for the design and construction
of a custom-made youth shelter. Glazzards were
involved in an innovative pilot programme, to
demonstrate the potential of effective and creative
community consultation and collaboration processes
in improving both the environment and people's lives.
1 2 3 4

GLAZZARD
ARCHITECTS

Next
Work
Home

Elmfield Rudolf Steiner School, Stourbridge
Design proposals for the remodelling of an existing
Victorian classroom building and the construction
of a new nursery/kindergarten unit.

The building is designed to provide maximum
flexibility and facilitate change with all walls being
non loadbearing partitions in order that spaces can
be opened-up and simply adapted as necessary.
Importance is given to the interplay between internal
and external teaching spaces and the buildings
relationship with the natural elements of the site.
1 2 3

GLAZZARD
ARCHITECTS

Next
Work
Home

Innovation Square, Birmingham
The mixed use scheme included the repair and
alterations to multiple listed buildings as well as
construction of several new buildings around a
central courtyard. At ground level a large structural
glass canopy leads to a dramatic entrance atrium
with scenic lift to all levels.
1 3

GLAZZARD
ARCHITECTS

Film and moving image | **Websites and hand-helds** | Industry view: Toko

Liquid layout

A liquid, or flexible layout is one where the elements on the page move in relation to a viewer's browser. This means that as you contract or expand your browser, so too the size and position of elements on the page also shift and change. In the example above, the information is fixed at the top left of the browser, while the logo is fixed bottom right and the image element is flexible.

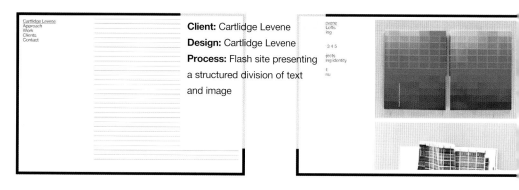

Client: Cartlidge Levene

Design: Cartlidge Levene

Process: Flash site presenting a structured division of text and image

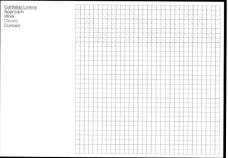

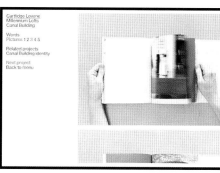

Cartlidge Levene

Cartlidge Levene, a renowned modernist typographic studio, designed a Flash website for itself in which the main window displays a sliver of the subsequent page as well as the current page. For example, in the portfolio section of the website, you can see part of the next image in addition to the image on the page. This controlled scroll effect provides a means of changing and optimizing the formatting constraints of the web browser.
www.cartlidgelevene.co.uk

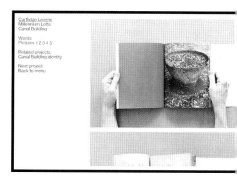

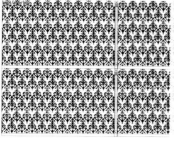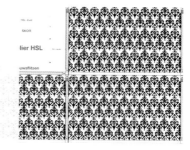

Client: Lust
Design: Lust
Process: HTML website challenging the way we perceive the display of information

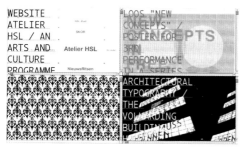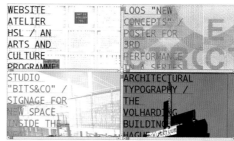

Lust

The website of Lust, a typography, design and propaganda design studio based in The Hague, the Netherlands, showcases Dutch graphic design. Lust has a philosophy that revolves around process-based design, coincidence and the degradation of form and content. In one section of its website, Lust formats the screen into four windows with standard clickable links in each that change the information presented in all four windows in a manner that is definitely not standard. www.lust.nl

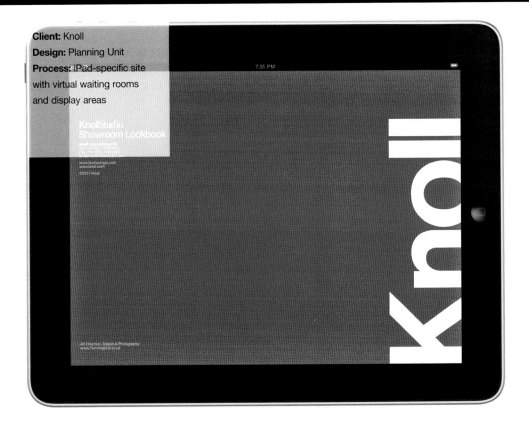

Client: Knoll

Design: Planning Unit

Process: iPad-specific site with virtual waiting rooms and display areas

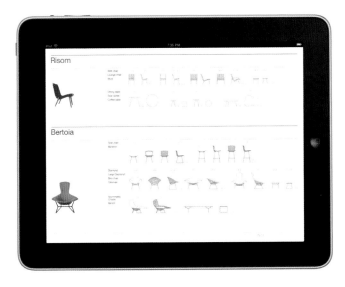

Knoll

Designed especially for Clerkenwell Design Week, London in 2011, this iPad lookbook demonstrates a confident use of colour and brand in a size-specific format. Shown above is the landing page, an expression of the brand's confidence and the virtual waiting area (page 187, top). This leads through to an index page (left).

Making appropriate use of the space and format is key to the success of a discrete site, in order to create an immersive environment and showcase products in an engaging way.

Client: Shpilman Institute
for Photography
Design: Planning Unit
Process: WordPress-driven
website, allowing multiple
users to update content

Shpilman Institute for Photography

Designed in WordPress, this website for the Shpilman Institute for Photography uses a core grid of five main sections. As the site is also viewable as a Hebrew version, the grid structure had to be equally effective in reverse. The site also uses a Content Management System (CMS), which means that the content can be changed regularly making a dynamic and active environment.
thesip.org

Content Management Systems (CMS)

Content Management Systems (CMS) allow multiple users to add content to a website. They also have the advantage of not requiring the user to have HTML or programming skills. Recently, platforms like WordPress, an open-source blog and publishing tool, have been widely customized to act as CMS.

Film and moving image | **Websites and hand-helds** | Industry view: Toko

Industry view: Toko

Toko's website for Australian fashion designer Alistair Trung demonstrates a strong sense of format and grid, while still remaining personal and delicate.

The structure of the site is both formal (structured) and fluid (dynamic and delicate). Is this combination something that you intentionally try to instil to humanize technology?

Absolutely, Alistair Trung's work has to be seen and touched to be fully appreciated for its amazing detail and quality. Digitizing his work would always involve a compromise but we tried to achieve a sense of calm and depth within the website to somehow emphasize the pure quality of his creations.

The site uses a combination of product, the design of Alistair Trung, and also reference and research material from the designer. Can you elaborate on how this combination of materials came together?

Part of the creative brief was a request for the inclusion of personality (not just a showcase of his latest collections), which we achieved by including those materials and quotes, so creating an honest reflection of Alistair both as a person and a designer.

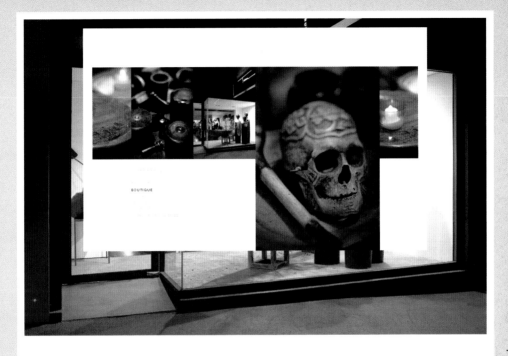

Fashion designer Alistair Trung's masterful creations are presented in a calm, delicate and considered way. Inspirational images, such as the skull above for example, act as a counterpoint to the final designs.

There's a strong sense of grid and juxtaposition of photography. Do you find that online work offers a difference in approach to the printed page – are there advantages or disadvantages?
Working in 'layers' and creating surprise is an absolute advantage of the digital but visualizing quality in depth will always be an issue.

Toko. Concept. Design. Established in 2002 in Rotterdam, the Netherlands, and since 2008 permanently operating out of Surry Hills, Sydney, Australia, Toko's creative output can be appreciated through an extensive portfolio of work realized for both national and international clients in a diverse range of fields, including The Powerhouse Museum, Virgin Atlantic, Architecture Institute Australia, SBS, MTV and The Communications Council. **www.toko.nu**

Design activity:
Multiple mediums

Premise
The advent of the Internet and new media means that products and services are presented over multiple mediums. This presents both problems and possibilities for a professional designer.

Exercise
1 Take a government health initiative (see below) and present an approach to how this message can work over the following mediums: a) printed leaflet, b) iPad-specific application, c) iPhone and d) website.

- *Government alcohol strategy* – the strategy sets out to: minimize the health harms, violence and antisocial behaviour associated with alcohol, while ensuring that people are able to enjoy alcohol safely and responsibly.

- *Violent Crime Action Plan and domestic violence* – the government's objective in relation to domestic violence is to roll out good practice developed in tackling domestic violence.

- *A Tobacco Control Plan* – to mark No Smoking Day, the government has announced plans to protect the public from the substantial dangers to health posed by tobacco.

2 Consider how the different mediums have unique qualities in terms of how we use them and the amount of copy that is appropriate for each. You need to consider how much time your audience will spend looking at your campaign – for example, a website can be more effective with less text.

Aim
To think about the differences (advantages and disadvantages) of different mediums.

Outcome
You have now gained experience of producing a campaign that works across multiple mediums.

Suggested reading
- *The Complete Guide to Digital Graphic Design* by Bob Gordon and Maggie Gordon (Thames & Hudson, 2005)
- *A Practical Guide to Digital Design: Designing With Your Computer Made Easy!* by Pina Lewandowsky and Francis Zeischegg (AVA Publishing, 2003)

Glossary

Accordion or concertina fold
Two or more parallel folds that go in opposite directions and open out like an accordion.

A series paper sizes
ISO metric standard paper size based on the square root of two ratio. The A0 sheet (841mm x 1189mm/46.8in x 33.1in) is one square metre and each size (A1, A2, A3, A4 etc.) then differs from the next by a factor of either 2 or $^1/_2$.

Basis weight
The weight, measured in pounds, of 500 sheets (a ream) of paper cut to a standard size.

Bellyband
A printed band that wraps around a publication, typically magazines.

Bible paper or India paper
A thin, lightweight, long-life, opaque paper grade typically made from 25% cotton and linen rags or flax with chemical wood pulp, named after its most common usage.

Binding
Any of several processes for holding together the pages or sections of a publication to form a book, magazine, brochure or some other format using stitches, wire, glue or other media.

Bleed printing
Printed information extends past where pages will be trimmed so that colours or images continue to the edge of the cut page.

Brittleness
Meaning easily broken, an important paper attribute to be aware of when considering folding as you do not want it to crack.

B series paper sizes
ISO metric standard paper size based on the square root of two ratio. B sizes are intermediate sizes to the A series sizes.

Buckram
A coarse linen or cotton fabric sized with glue or gum, used for covering a hard-cover binding.

Burst binding
At the folding stage the sections are perforated on the binding side to allow glue to penetrate into each fold of paper. The glued spine then has a cover applied and wrapped around the book block.

Canadian binding
Essentially a spiral-bound volume with a wrap-around cover that can stand up better on a shelf, with a spine for the title. A half-Canadian has an exposed spiral, a full Canadian does not.

Case or edition binding
A common hard-cover book-binding method that sews signatures together, flattens the spine, and applies endsheets and head and tail bands to the spine. Hard covers are attached, the spine is usually rounded and grooves along the cover edge act as hinges.

Concertina fold
See Accordion fold.

Crack-back
A backing stock with a self-adhesive coating that may have a die cut to make it easier to peel away from the stock it backs.

Creasing
A blade and pressure are used to impart a crease into a substrate so that it can later be folded. Similar to a die cut but the blade does not penetrate the substrate.

Creep
Creep occurs in a saddle-stitched publication when the bulk of the paper causes the inner pages to extend (creep) further than the outer pages when folded.

Cross fold
Two or more folds going in different directions, typically at right angles. Mainly used in book work where paper is cross folded and cut to form a signature.

Deboss
As emboss but recessed into the substrate.

Deckle or feather edge
The ragged edge of the paper as it comes from the papermaking machine. Machine-made paper has two deckle edges, handmade has four. When not cut off it can serve a decorative purpose. An imitation deckle edge can be created by tearing the edge of the paper.

Die cut

Special shapes cut in a substrate by a steel die.

Double gatefold

Three panels that fold into the middle of a publication, slightly smaller in width to the inner panels so that when folded they can nest inside the publication.

Duotone

A two-colour reproduction from a monochrome original.

Dust jacket

A jacket around a hardback publication that originally offered protection against dirt and dust, as the name suggests, but more recently has become an integral graphic extension of the book and a key device for promotion.

Emboss

A design stamped without ink or foil giving a raised surface.

Endpaper or endsheets

The heavy cartridge paper pages at the front and back of a hardback book that join the book block to the hardback binding. Sometimes feature maps, a decorative colour or design.

Extent

The number of pages in a book.

Fan fold

A fan fold or accordion fold is a series of parallel folds made in the opposite direction to the previous fold along its length and then one right-angle fold to create a fan.

Flash

Animation software that enables web pages to be brought to life in the most remarkable ways and with a high degree of sophistication.

Flock

A speciality cover paper produced by coating the sheet with size in patterns or all over, after which a dyed flock powder (very fine woollen refuse or vegetable fibre dust) is applied. Originally intended to simulate tapestry and Italian velvet brocade.

Flood colour

A term referring to the colour fill of an item.

Foil, heat or hot stamp

Foil pressed on to a substrate using heat and pressure. Also known as block print or foil emboss.

Folio or page

A sheet of paper folded in half is a folio and each half of the folio is one page. A single folio has four pages.

French fold

A sheet of paper that is only printed on one side and folded with two right-angle folds to form a four-page, uncut section. The section is sewn through the fold while the top edges remain folded and untrimmed.

Frontispiece

An illustration inserted to face the title page.

Gatefold

The left and right edges fold inward with parallel folds and meet in the middle of the page without overlapping.

Grain

Paper grain is the direction in which most of its fibres lay and is determined during the papermaking process. The grain flows in the direction that the paper passes through the papermaking machine.

Imposition

The arrangement of pages in the sequence and position they will appear when printed before being cut, folded and trimmed.

International Paper Sizes (ISO)

A range of standard metric paper sizes.

Japanese or stab binding

A binding method whereby the pages are sewn together with one continual thread.

Kiss cut

A method of die cutting whereby the face material of a self-adhesive substrate is die cut but not completely through to the backing sheet. This enables the face material to be easily removed from the backing sheet.

Laminate

A laminate is a stock made by bonding two or more layers of stock together. Typically used to provide a thick cover stock comprising a cheap inner with a printable outer.

Loose-leaf binding

A binding method in which individual, punched sheets are loosely held by a binder.

Litho

A printing technique in which the ink is transferred from a printing plate to a 'blanket' cylinder and then to the paper or material on which it is to be printed.

Perfect binding

A binding method commonly used for paperback books where the signatures are held together with a flexible adhesive that also attaches a paper cover to the spine. The fore-edge is trimmed flat.

Perforation

A series of cuts or holes manufactured on a form to weaken it for tearing.

Ream

500 sheets of paper.

Recto / Verso

The pages of an open book with recto being the right-hand page and verso the left-hand.

Saddle-stitching

A binding method used for booklets, programmes and small catalogues. Signatures are nested and wire stitches are applied through the spine along the centrefold. When opened, saddle-stitched books lay flat.

Showthrough or strikethrough

Where printing inks can be seen through the substrate on the reverse of the page. Particularly common with thin paper stocks and/or those with low loadings of fillers and coating; it is generally undesirable.

Side-stitching

A binding method for publications that are too bulky for saddle-stitching. Signatures are collated, placed flat under the stitching head and stapled. Side-stitched items do not lay flat when open.

Signature or section

A signature or section is a sheet of paper folded to form several pages which are collected together for binding.

Slipcase

A protective case for a book or set of books open at one end so that only the book spines are visible.

Stock

The paper to be printed upon.

Substrate

The material or surface to be printed upon.

Surrealism

A style of art and literature developed in the 20th century that stressed the subconscious or non-rational significance of imagery arrived at by automatism or the exploitation of chance effects and incongruous juxtapositions.

Tip-in

To attach an insert in a book or magazine by gluing along the binding edge such as to tip-in a colour plate.

UV coating

Coating applied to a printed substrate that is bonded and cured with ultraviolet light.

Varnish

A clear or tinted liquid shellac or plastic coating put on a printed piece to add a glossy, satin or dull finish applied like a final ink layer after a piece is printed (see front cover).

Vellum

Vellum is commonly used to mean a translucent paper although it can also mean a slightly rough paper finish.

Wiro/comb binding

A spine of plastic or wire rings that binds a document and allows it to open flat.

Z-bind

A 'z' shaped cover that is used to join two separate publications.

Acknowledgements and picture credits

We would like to thank everyone who supported us during this second edition including the many art directors, designers and creatives who showed great generosity in allowing us to reproduce their work. Special thanks to everyone that hunted for, collated, compiled and rediscovered some of the fascinating work contained in this book. Thanks to Xavier Young for his patience, determination and skill in photographing the work showcased in this book and to Heather Marshall for modelling. And a final big thanks to all the staff at AVA Publishing who never tired of our requests, enquiries and questions, and supported us throughout. We would especially like to thank Colette Meacher, who has helped collate and craft this second edition, building on the hard work that went into the original.

Lavernia & Cienfuegos Diseño (72, 126–127) Copyright © 2003–2012 Lavernia-Cienfuegos

Propaganda (170–172) © Propaganda

Planning Unit (186-187, 188-189, 146-148) © Planning Unit

Morse Studio (130–131, 140–141, 168–169) © Morse Studio

Andreas Roth (178–179) © Filmakademie Baden Württemberg

The Collective Design Consultants Pty Ltd (139, 142–143) © The Collective

Toko. Concept. Design. (68-69, 70–71, 190–192) © Alistair Trung. Photography: Emmanuel Giraud. Web development: Toko

The Design Shop (28–29) © the design shop

velladesign (76–78, 167) © Andy Vella/ Foruli Publishing

All reasonable attempts have been made to trace, clear and credit the copyright holders of the images reproduced in this book. However, if any credits have been inadvertently omitted, the publisher will endeavour to incorporate amendments in future editions.

Glossary | **Acknowledgements and picture credits** | Index

Index

Contacts

BASICS
DESIGN

Lynne Elvins
Naomi Goulder

Working with ethics

Publisher's note

The subject of ethics is not new, yet its consideration within the applied visual arts is perhaps not as prevalent as it might be. Our aim here is to help a new generation of students, educators and practitioners find a methodology for structuring their thoughts and reflections in this vital area.

AVA Publishing hopes that these **Working with ethics** pages provide a platform for consideration and a flexible method for incorporating ethical concerns in the work of educators, students and professionals. Our approach consists of four parts:

The **introduction** is intended to be an accessible snapshot of the ethical landscape, both in terms of historical development and current dominant themes.

The **framework** positions ethical consideration into four areas and poses questions about the practical implications that might occur. Marking your response to each of these questions on the scale shown will allow your reactions to be further explored by comparison.

The **case study** sets out a real project and then poses some ethical questions for further consideration. This is a focus point for a debate rather than a critical analysis so there are no predetermined right or wrong answers.

A selection of **further reading** for you to consider areas of particular interest in more detail.

Ethical: aware-ness/ reflect-ion/ debate

Working with ethics

Introduction

Ethics is a complex subject that interlaces the idea of responsibilities to society with a wide range of considerations relevant to the character and happiness of the individual. It concerns virtues of compassion, loyalty and strength, but also of confidence, imagination, humour and optimism. As introduced in ancient Greek philosophy, the fundamental ethical question is: *what should I do?* How we might pursue a 'good' life not only raises moral concerns about the effects of our actions on others, but also personal concerns about our own integrity.

In modern times the most important and controversial questions in ethics have been the moral ones. With growing populations and improvements in mobility and communications, it is not surprising that considerations about how to structure our lives together on the planet should come to the forefront. For visual artists and communicators, it should be no surprise that these considerations will enter into the creative process.

Some ethical considerations are already enshrined in government laws and regulations or in professional codes of conduct. For example, plagiarism and breaches of confidentiality can be punishable offences. Legislation in various nations makes it unlawful to exclude people with disabilities from accessing information or spaces. The trade of ivory as a material has been banned in many countries. In these cases, a clear line has been drawn under what is unacceptable.

But most ethical matters remain open to debate, among experts and lay-people alike, and in the end we have to make our own choices on the basis of our own guiding principles or values. Is it more ethical to work for a charity than for a commercial company? Is it unethical to create something that others find ugly or offensive?

Specific questions such as these may lead to other questions that are more abstract. For example, is it only effects on humans (and what they care about) that are important, or might effects on the natural world require attention too?

Is promoting ethical consequences justified even when it requires ethical sacrifices along the way? Must there be a single unifying theory of ethics (such as the Utilitarian thesis that the right course of action is always the one that leads to the greatest happiness of the greatest number), or might there always be many different ethical values that pull a person in various directions?

As we enter into ethical debate and engage with these dilemmas on a personal and professional level, we may change our views or change our view of others. The real test though is whether, as we reflect on these matters, we change the way we act as well as the way we think. Socrates, the 'father' of philosophy, proposed that people will naturally do 'good' if they know what is right. But this point might only lead us to yet another question: *how do we know what is right?*

You
What are your ethical beliefs?

Central to everything you do will be your attitude to people and issues around you. For some people, their ethics are an active part of the decisions they make every day as a consumer, a voter or a working professional. Others may think about ethics very little and yet this does not automatically make them unethical. Personal beliefs, lifestyle, politics, nationality, religion, gender, class or education can all influence your ethical viewpoint.

Using the scale, where would you place yourself? What do you take into account to make your decision? Compare results with your friends or colleagues.

Your client
What are your terms?

Working relationships are central to whether ethics can be embedded into a project, and your conduct on a day-to-day basis is a demonstration of your professional ethics. The decision with the biggest impact is whom you choose to work with in the first place. Cigarette companies or arms traders are often-cited examples when talking about where a line might be drawn, but rarely are real situations so extreme. At what point might you turn down a project on ethical grounds and how much does the reality of having to earn a living affect your ability to choose?

Using the scale, where would you place a project? How does this compare to your personal ethical level?

01 02 03 04 05 06 07 08 09 10

01 02 03 04 05 06 07 08 09 10

Your specifications

What are the impacts of your
materials?

In relatively recent times, we are
learning that many natural materials
are in short supply. At the same
time, we are increasingly aware that
some man-made materials can have
harmful, long-term effects on people
or the planet. How much do you know
about the materials that you use?
Do you know where they come from,
how far they travel and under what
conditions they are obtained? When
your creation is no longer needed,
will it be easy and safe to recycle? Will
it disappear without a trace? Are these
considerations your responsibility or
are they out of your hands?

Using the scale, mark how ethical
your material choices are.

Your creation

What is the purpose of your work?

Between you, your colleagues
and an agreed brief, what will your
creation achieve? What purpose
will it have in society and will it make
a positive contribution? Should your
work result in more than commercial
success or industry awards? Might
your creation help save lives, educate,
protect or inspire? Form and function
are two established aspects of judging
a creation, but there is little consensus
on the obligations of visual artists
and communicators toward society,
or the role they might have in solving
social or environmental problems.
If you want recognition for being the
creator, how responsible are you for
what you create and where might that
responsibility end?

Using the scale, mark how ethical the
purpose of your work is.

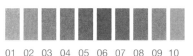

01 02 03 04 05 06 07 08 09 10

01 02 03 04 05 06 07 08 09 10

Working with ethics

One aspect of graphic design that raises an ethical dilemma is that of its relationship with the creation of printed materials and the environmental impacts of print production. For example, in the UK, it is estimated that around 5.4 billion items of addressed direct mail are sent out every year and these, along with other promotional inserts, amount to over half a million tonnes of paper annually (almost 5 per cent of the UK consumption of paper and board). Response rates to mail campaigns are known to be between 1–3 per cent, making junk mail arguably one of the least environmentally friendly forms of print communication. As well as the use of paper or board, the design decisions to use scratch-off panels, heavily coated gloss finishes, full-colour ink-intensive graphics or glues for seals or fixings make paper more difficult to recycle once it has been discarded. How much responsibility should a graphic designer have in this situation if a client has already chosen to embark on a direct mail campaign and has a format in mind? Even if designers wish to minimise the environmental impacts of print materials, what might they most usefully do?

In 1951, Leo Burnett (the famous advertising executive known for creating the Jolly Green Giant and the Marlboro Man) was hired to create a campaign for Kellogg's new cereal, Sugar Frosted Flakes (now Frosties in the UK and Frosted Flakes in the US). Tony the Tiger, designed by children's book illustrator Martin Provensen, was one of four characters selected to sell the cereal. Newt the Gnu and Elmo the Elephant never made it to the shelves and after Tony proved more popular than Katy the Kangaroo, she was dropped from packs after the first year.

Whilst the orange-and-black tiger stripes and the red kerchief have remained, Provensen's original design for Tony has changed significantly since he first appeared in 1952. Tony started out with an American football-shaped head, which later became more rounded, and his eye colour changed from green to gold. Today, his head is more angular and he sits on a predominantly blue background. Tony was initially presented as a character that walked on all fours and was no bigger than a cereal box. By the 1970s, Tony's physique had developed into a slim and muscular six-foot-tall standing figure.

Between 1952 and 1995 Kellogg's are said to have spent more than USD$1 billion promoting Frosted Flakes with Tony's image, while generating USD$5.3 billion in gross US sales But surveys by consumer rights groups such as Which? find that over 75 per cent of people believe that using characters on packaging makes it hard for parents to say no to their children. In these surveys, Kellogg's come under specific scrutiny for Frosties, which are said to contain one third sugar and more salt than the Food Standards Agency recommends. In response, Kellogg's have said: 'We are committed to responsibly marketing our brands and communicating their intrinsic qualities so that our customers can make informed choices.'

Food campaigners claim that the use of cartoon characters is a particularly manipulative part of the problem and governments should stop them being used on less healthy children's foods. But in 2008, spokespeople for the Food and Drink Federation in the UK, said: 'We are baffled as to why Which? wants to take all the fun out of food by banning popular brand characters, many of whom have been adding colour to supermarket shelves for more than 80 years.'

Is it more ethical to create promotional graphics for 'healthy' rather than 'unhealthy' food products?

Is it unethical to design cartoon characters to appeal to children for commercial purposes?

Would you have worked on this project, either now or in the 1950s?

I studied graphic design in Germany, and my professor emphasised the responsibility that designers and illustrators have towards the people they create things for.

Eric Carle
(illustrator)

AIGA
Design Business and Ethics
2007, AIGA

Eaton, Marcia Muelder
Aesthetics and the Good Life
1989, Associated University Press

Ellison, David
Ethics and Aesthetics in European Modernist Literature:
From the Sublime to the Uncanny
2001, Cambridge University Press

Fenner, David E W (Ed)
Ethics and the Arts:
An Anthology
1995, Garland Reference Library of Social Science

Gini, Al and Marcoux, Alexei M
Case Studies in Business Ethics
2005, Prentice Hall

McDonough, William and Braungart, Michael
Cradle to Cradle:
Remaking the Way We Make Things
2002, North Point Press

Papanek, Victor
Design for the Real World:
Making to Measure
1972, Thames & Hudson

United Nations Global Compact
The Ten Principles
www.unglobalcompact.org/AboutTheGC/TheTenPrinciples/index.html